"IQ tests measure *something*. The problem is what to call it."
Jeremy Berenstein

Grammatix, Inc.

presents

the COMPLETE

SAT AND PSAT STRATEGY GUIDE

This Strategy Guide contains EVERYTHING you need to know to maximize your SAT score in as little time as possible. These guides will show you how to use hidden rules and patterns to tear the tests apart. So get ready to see the SAT and PSAT in a whole new light!

Visit Grammatix on the web at www.grammatix.com.

Grammatix
JACKSONVILLE, FLORIDA

Manufactured in the United States of America.

ISBN 0-9721161-6-8

A Special Message to the Reader

What you are about to read will teach you a totally fresh, systematic, and learnable way to attack SAT and PSAT questions. This approach is very different from the traditional approach taught by other test prep companies. For one thing, it's faster and much more simplified. For another, it actually works.

Forget what other people have told you about the SAT and PSAT. This Strategy Guide will show you a better way. Soon, you'll be answering questions just like natural test-takers!

The writer of this guide is an experienced test prep instructor who developed these methods so that all test-takers could earn higher scores. These ideas and techniques have been "battle-tested" in real classroom situations with real students, and they've proven themselves time and again.

Now it's your turn to learn these simple, fast techniques and turn yourself into a natural test-taker!

Thank you for your purchase, and congratulations!

THE PUBLISHER

Table Of Contents

How To Use This Strategy Guide

What you're holding in your hand is the absolute best source of SAT strategies available anywhere. This Strategy Guide contains every single piece of information you need to beat the SAT. If you're willing to read this Guide and keep an open mind, you can raise your SAT score. That's all there is to it.

This Strategy Guide consists of six Question-Type Guides and several special sections. The six Question Type Guides show you how to attack specific question types on the SAT. They follow this general format, which has been designed and tested to provide as much information as possible in as little time as possible:

- General Overview of Each Question Type
- The Rules for Each Question Type
- The Hidden Patterns of Each Question Type
- Special Techniques for Each Question Type
- The Recommended Completion Process for Each Question Type
- Using the Recommended Completion Process

The guides for the SAT Math and SAT Writing questions also include "Toolboxes," which are quick-reference sections that give you all the background you need to answer any SAT Math or Writing question.

Sections Of Each Question-Type Guide

The purposes of the different sections of each Question-Type Guide are explained below.

General Overview of Each Question Type

The General Overview explains how each type of SAT question works. It discusses common misconceptions that affect student performance on the particular question types, and introduces the basic tools you'll need to answer those questions.

The Rules for Each Question Type

This section explains the unwritten rules that you absolutely must understand in order to answer a particular type of SAT question.

The Hidden Patterns of Each Question Type

Natural test-takers use hidden patterns to identify correct answers to SAT Questions. This section shows you the most important patterns on the test, so you can use them to make all SAT questions easier.

The Recommended Completion Process for Each Question Type

In this section, you learn new processes you can use to answer any SAT question.

Using the Recommended Completion Process

The best way to learn any process is to see it in action. This section shows you how the SAT Completion Processes can be used to answer REAL questions from actual SATs. You can find these real question in the College Board publication *The Official SAT Study Guide For The New SAT*.

Supplementary Materials

The section of each Strategy Guide entitled "Using the Process" is designed to accompany a copy of *The Official SAT Study Guide For The New SAT*. *The Official SAT Study Guide For The New SAT* is a publication of College Entrance Examination Board and Educational Testing Service, which has no affiliation of any kind with Grammatix, Inc.

The Official SAT Study Guide For The New SAT contains copies of sample SAT examinations prepared by the company that writes the SAT, which are absolutely necessary for thorough preparation. If you don't have a copy of *The Official SAT Study Guide For The New SAT*, you can get one from the library or from a bookstore.

Important Icons

Throughout these Strategy Guides, two icons are used to get your attention.

This icon appears when I talk about strategies, tricks, and tips that are especially effective.

This icon appears when I talk about specific points that are crucial to your success.

All Grammatix Strategy Guides are packed with information, so read every word! These icons appear when I want to make absolutely certain that you're paying attention!

Using This Guide To Prepare For The PSAT

With the changes that were made to the PSAT and SAT in 2004 and 2005, the two tests became much more similar than they were before. This makes it much easier for you to prepare for the PSAT without wasting any time.

Basically, the only important differences between the PSAT and the SAT are these:

- The PSAT does NOT include an essay portion, and
- PSAT math is NOT as advanced as SAT Math.

www.grammatix.com

So, as a practical matter, the best way to prepare for the PSAT is simply to prepare for the SAT as you normally would—the PSAT will probably seem much easier in comparison. If you don't have much time before the PSAT and you haven't started preparing for the SAT yet, then you can leave out the essay portion of your SAT prep and only focus on the parts of the SAT that will appear on the PSAT.

Now let's get started with our first Question-Type Guide!

READ THIS FIRST!

If you're reading this Strategy Guide, it's probably because you don't feel that you're adequately prepared to take the SAT. (If you felt prepared, you wouldn't need to keep preparing.)

You've probably started preparing with other SAT materials before using this Guide, or at least received some SAT advice from friends, teachers, or counselors. If that's the case, you'll probably notice two things about the Strategy Guide you're reading right now:

- It often contradicts the advice and strategies you're already familiar with, and
- It's more simple and straightforward than other advice and strategies.

Don't reject the advice in this Strategy Guide because it's different from what you've already learned! We've already established that what you've already learned hasn't gotten you the score you wanted—otherwise you wouldn't be reading this.

I beg you, for your own sake, to keep an open mind when reading this Guide. It's different from other stuff you've already read. It's faster and more effective.

For some reason, when people find this out, they often assume that my approach can't possibly work. I can't tell you how many times I've been asked this question:

> "If your approach is so much better, why hasn't a big test prep company come up with it already?

Honestly, I don't have any idea why nobody has come up with my approach before. Why not ask the United States Post Office why it didn't invent email? It doesn't matter why I'm the first one to come out with such an effective SAT guide. It only matters that the approach in this Strategy Guide is uniquely effective and easy to learn, and if you've had problems getting the SAT score you want, I can help you overcome them.

But remember—this Strategy Guide won't make any difference to your score if you don't read it with an open mind and work to apply the strategies in these pages. If you just read through this Guide absent-mindedly and then go right back to all your old, bad habits, you won't see any improvement. Trust me on this.

Now, we need to talk about two important aspects of using this guide: skipping what you don't need, and testing what you don't agree with.

Skipping What You Don't Need

When using this Strategy Guide (or any other SAT advice), it's important not to waste time where you don't need to. In other words, if you're happy with your performance on a particular question type, don't bother learning a new approach to it! If you feel like your Math score is already where you want it, then focus on improving your Writing and Critical Reading skills. It doesn't make any sense to clutter your mind with new ways to do something you already know how to do.

Of course, if none of your scores are quite where you want them—which is probably the case—then you should work on every section of the test until you're happy with your scores.

Testing What You Don't Agree With

If you've used any other SAT prep materials, you probably have your own ideas about the best way to approach the test. That's perfectly okay. But there will be times in this Strategy Guide when I'll say something you disagree with.

When that happens, do us both a favor—test it out! Don't just dismiss my advice without giving it a try first. That isn't fair to either of us. If you don't put ALL the advice you receive to the test, you'll never know if you're using the best strategies. You'll end up doing what almost everybody else does—following the same old traditional advice because everyone has always followed it. And you'll end up with an average SAT score, and you won't know why.

When you test out any SAT advice, be sure you use only real SAT sample tests prepared by the College Board itself. Don't trust a sample test prepared by a big test prep company or some third-party web site—those questions aren't designed according to the same standards as real SAT questions, and they won't tell you anything meaningful about what the test is really like.

A Word On Guessing: Don't.

We need to clear something up before we even start talking about taking the SAT.

If you've ever been given any advice at all about how to take the SAT, it probably included this little pearl:

"If you ever get stumped on a question, just try to eliminate one or two answers and then guess from the rest."

It's the single most popular test-taking strategy of all time. Your friends have heard it. Every test prep company uses it. Your guidance counselors might have told you about it. Even the College Board tells you to do it. And as it turns out, it's an absolutely awful piece of advice in almost every case. Let's take a closer look at it.

First Things First: Guessing Defined

Before we can talk about why guessing on the SAT is bad, we have to make sure we're talking about the same thing when we use the word *guessing*. When I talk about guessing, I'm talking about marking an answer choice on a multiple-choice question without being certain that the answer choice I'm marking is correct.

I'm NOT necessarily talking about marking an answer choice when I don't know the meaning of every word in the question, when I don't know what a sentence says, when I'm not sure of my grammar, when I don't know for certain how to do the math involved, or anything like that.

Can you see the difference? Natural test-takers encounter things they don't know or have never heard of every time they take the SAT. It's totally normal. In fact, in a lot of ways it's inevitable—the non-math questions, especially, can be about almost anything, even though their structures have to follow the rules and patterns of the test. But if you know the test (and you will know it if you've studied this guide), you can still choose the correct answer choice reliably EVEN THOUGH YOU DON'T KNOW EVERYTHING IN THE QUESTION. In this case, for our purposes, you are NOT guessing—guessing only happens when you're not sure the answer you're marking is right. For our purposes, guessing has nothing to do with whether you understand the question you're being asked, and everything to do with whether you're certain the answer you mark is correct.

It's very important that you understand this distinction before we continue the discussion; otherwise, you might think I'm telling you to give up whenever you come to a question you don't understand fully, which is absolutely NOT what I'm telling you to do.

Now that we've gotten that straightened out, let's talk about why people guess on the SAT in the first place.

The Argument For Guessing

The argument for guessing on the SAT relies on the way the test is designed. As you may know, you get a single raw point for every correct answer to a multiple-choice question on the SAT. You lose a fraction of a raw point for each wrong answer to a multiple-choice question. This fractional loss is set up so that if you guess randomly on every single question on the test, you should come out with a total score of 0 raw points.

How can that be? Well, for a five-answer multiple-choice question, you'll get a full raw point if you're correct and you'll lose a quarter of a raw point if you're wrong. So if you guess randomly, in any five questions with five answers each, you should get one correct answer and four incorrect answers—which comes out to a net score of 0 raw points.

The argument for guessing tries to change those odds. According to the guessing theory, if you could remove one or two answer choices from each question, and then guess randomly from what you had left, you should be able to beat the test and get a few extra raw points. The thinking works like this: If you can remove two answer choices for each question, then you should only really be guessing from three answer choices on each five-answer question. If you guess from three answer choices, you should be right every third time (instead of only being right every fifth time, which is what you would expect if you didn't remove any answer choices at all). But you'll still only be penalized one-fourth of a raw point for being wrong. Over time, guessing correctly every three tries and only being penalized as though you were guessing correctly every fifth time, you should come out ahead.

If you've done other SAT prep before, you've probably heard this argument before. You might even be nodding in agreement. It's simple probability, right?

Wrong.

This is an example of *over-simplified* probability. The argument for guessing on the SAT assumes two things that just plain aren't true in real life.

The Problem With Guessing

In order for the argument for guessing to be any good, two things would have to happen:
1. You have to eliminate only incorrect answer choices.
2. You have to guess randomly from the remaining answer choices.

Do you see why this is?

In the first place, if you eliminate the correct answer choice from the pool of possible answers you'll consider, then how likely are you to get the question right by picking the eliminated answer? You're not likely to at all. In fact, you can't do it. It's impossible to pick an answer choice that you've eliminated from the guessing.

As for the second assumption, if you don't guess randomly, then the entire argument about what "should" happen according to "probability" goes right out the window. There's no probability involved at all if you don't make a completely random guess. (Making a guess where you consider the validity of each answer choice isn't random. "Random" means you don't interfere at all. For example, flipping a penny in the air to see how many times it comes up heads is random; catching it every time before it lands and setting it down tails-up destroys the randomness by interfering with the process. That's essentially what you're doing if you consider whether the answer choices are any good or not.)

---

www.grammatix.com

What Really Happens

Most of the people who employ the classic so-called "guessing" strategy are actually doing something very different from eliminating incorrect answers and then making a random, impartial guess. So what are they really doing, and why doesn't it work?

When people who follow the guessing strategy come to a question they can't answer, the first thing they usually do is look for an answer choice they like. Then they look to see if they can find one or two other answer choices to "eliminate." And that's it—they've basically used a bad theory based on a bad argument to justify marking a wrong answer. And, as a result, they lose raw points left and right. They'd be much better off just leaving those questions blank.

Why Guessing Fails On The SAT

There's a reason it's almost impossible to satisfy the two assumptions of the guessing strategy. The SAT is intentionally written so that incorrect answer choices seem like correct answer choices to people who don't know how to answer the questions. In other words, the very thing that keeps you from understanding a question in the first place is also the thing that will keep you from (1) eliminating only wrong answers, and (2) making an impartial guess from the remaining choices.

What does all this mean? On the SAT, in order to use the classical "guessing" strategy effectively, you have to be wrong about why you're wrong. Which can be difficult.

(Here's a coincidence that borders on conspiracy: as previously noted, the College Board endorses the guessing strategy described above. And the College Board is also the group that writes SAT questions so that incorrect answer choices look like correct ones—which makes good guessing almost impossible. Hmmmm . . .)

What You Should Do Instead

So if you don't use the guessing strategy, what should you do instead? Simple. When you come to a question and you can't figure out the answer, skip it. Don't think about it. Just do it. Remember, the only real alternative is to put down a wrong answer and lose points.

It takes discipline to leave a question blank on an important test like the SAT. But you have to do it. If you really can't figure out the answer, there's no better choice than skipping the question.

I'll repeat this again to make sure I'm being crystal-clear: if you can't figure out an answer, skip the question. That's all.

Proof That Guessing Is Bad

If you're like most people, you probably don't believe me when I say that SAT guessing is a bad idea. You've probably been told by almost everyone you know that you should eliminate the incorrect answer choices and guess from the remaining choices whenever you get stumped on the SAT. And the argument in support of guessing seems fairly seductive and clever, I'll admit—until you examine the two things it relies on, at which point the argument falls apart for most people.

www.grammatix.com

How can I prove what I'm saying? There are two ways. The first way is by pointing out that high-scorers (99th percentile and above) never guess. Find some and ask them. In my years of SAT experience, having discussed the situation with literally thousands of people, I've encountered one student who said he followed the traditional guessing strategy and scored even above 1400 on the old SAT (which was measured on a 1600 scale at the time). One. And after talking to him about it a little, it became clear that he wasn't really "guessing" in the sense that the College Board recommends you guess. Instead, he was more often using a logical process of elimination to arrive at a correct answer choice—something that all natural test-takers do, and something that doesn't fall under the definition of guessing that I explained above.

But the second way to prove that guessing is a bad idea is much better, and much more relevant to you as an individual. Just take a sample test from the College Board publication *The Official SAT Study Guide For The New SAT*, and make a note on your answer sheet every time you mark an answer you're not sure of. Then, when you add up your score, calculate it first with all the questions included, and compare this to the score you would have received if you had omitted the questions where you weren't sure of the answers. You will almost certainly find that your score is higher when you omit the questions you guessed on.

If this is NOT what you find, there are two possible reasons. It might be that you're one of the few people on Earth who actually guesses well using the classical strategy, in which case you should count yourself lucky and write a thank-you letter to the College Board. The more likely explanation is that you're still scoring lower than you want to, and you haven't spent enough time with the Grammatix processes and strategies for them to make a difference in your score—you haven't spent enough time to develop a real sense of certainty about when you're right and when you're guessing. As you'll see, the higher your score goes, the less guessing you'll find that you do. People simply don't guess their way into a top score on the SAT.

The Origins Of Traditional Guessing

So if the traditional guessing strategy is such a flawed idea, where did it come from? Good question. I think there are two possible explanations.

First, major test prep companies need a piece of fall-back advice they can give to their students, and this must seem like a pretty good one. With this one strategy, even a person who had learned nothing at all from an 8-week class could feel empowered to tackle any SAT question and stand a decent chance of improving his score. And since the major test prep companies write their own practice questions, they can construct those questions so that certain answer choices are obviously incorrect—which isn't how real SAT questions are written, but who'll ever notice?

Second, the College Board itself must have a stake in perpetuating the traditional guessing approach. It's been a part of their official advice for years now. But let's think for a moment—in 2004 and 2005, the College Board came under heavy fire for the SAT and made several large-scale changes to the old version of the test. They cut out whole question types, added an entire section, changed the essay instrument from the old SAT Writing II essay, and added new content to the Math section, among other things. They did these things mostly because some colleges and universities—the College Board's clients, in a way—complained about the old test design and what it showed (or didn't show) about a student's abilities.

www.grammatix.com

Now, we can be pretty sure that if there had been a problem with students guessing their way to higher scores, the College Board would have addressed the situation during its latest major overhaul. They didn't. If the College Board knew about the guessing strategy, and if that strategy worked so well, why didn't they change the test to make it impossible? And while we're at it, why do they keep telling their students to use it? I'll leave the answers up to you.

Conclusion

Guessing on the SAT is almost certainly a losing proposition for you. Test it out and see for yourself. The best thing to do when you come to a question you can't answer is to skip it. I know it's hard, but it sure beats losing points!

(For more on knowing when to skip an answer, see "No Two Ways About It" in this Guide.)

Remember that "guessing" only refers to the act of marking an answer when you're not sure that the answer is correct. On the SAT, there are ways to know your answer is correct even when you don't completely understand the question. Marking an answer choice in that situation isn't guessing—it's smart, natural test-taking!

Grammatix, Inc.

presents

how to attack
SAT Essay
Writing
like a natural test-taker

This Question-Type Guide will take all the mystery out of writing a top-scoring essay for the SAT. You'll learn what the SAT graders really look for (instead of what they claim to look for), and you'll see a "perfect" SAT essay put together right in front of you.

www.grammatix.com

General Overview of the SAT Essay

The essay on the SAT is supposed to evaluate your ability to produce "good writing." The College Board's intention here is commendable, but the essay test it has come up with is an awful tool for measuring writing ability. In other words, while a good writer should score well on this writing exercise, it's very possible to score well without being a good writer at all.

All you have to do is imitate (almost copy) the high-scoring sample essays from the College Board publication *The Official SAT Study Guide For the New SAT.* In the coming pages, you'll see exactly what sets apart a high-scoring essay, and exactly how to construct one of your very own.

While you should do your best to imitate high-scoring sample essays and copy their techniques, you should NEVER plagiarize ANYTHING, ever. We're not suggesting that you recycle any passage from anyone else's work as your own. For one thing, since SAT essay topics aren't repeated, it's unlikely that an exact passage from a high-scoring sample essay will help you much; more importantly, though, passing off another person's work as your own is one of the most reprehensible things anyone can do. So don't do it.

The Rules for the SAT Essay

Believe it or not, even essay tests have rules. You have to learn them if you want to do well. But be careful! The SAT Scoring Guide that appears on page 105 of the College Board Publication *The Official SAT Study Guide For the New SAT* isn't very useful if you're trying to figure out exactly what to do on the test.

It might sound strange to say this, but most of the College Board's advice on how to write the SAT essay is very, very bad. Instead of following the rules that the College Board states explicitly, we'll do something much smarter—we'll figure out the rules that are implicitly revealed in the high- and low-scoring sample responses provided by the College Board in *The Official SAT Study Guide For the New SAT*. Here they are.

 Remember that these are the rules revealed by actual high- and low-scoring sample essays released by the College Board. As such, they may be very different from the stated rules that you'll find on page 105, and elsewhere, in *The Official SAT Study Guide For the New SAT*.

SAT Essay Rule 1: Open-Ended Prompts

The prompts that appear on the SAT Writing Test are all open-ended and fairly vague about what they want you to write. This gives you a wide degree of latitude in deciding what to write, which can be a good thing if you don't let it overwhelm you.

SAT Essay Rule 2: Talk About Whatever You Want

When you plan your answer, you don't have to worry about being politically correct or trying not to offend your reader. Don't believe me? Take a look at page 197 of the College Board publication *The Official SAT Study Guide For The New SAT*. You'll see a top-scoring essay that talks favorably about how the Confederate Army was "defending its way of life" during the Civil War.

Now, nobody is suggesting that you go out of your way to discuss something controversial or offensive. All we're trying to point out is that there's no need to be worried that you might say the wrong thing. As the essay on page 197 demonstrates, the graders are interested in how well you develop an argument that relates to the prompt— they don't really care what the argument actually is.

SAT Essay Rule 3: Make Up Any Proof You Want

When you're looking for examples to support your argument, the SAT allows you to draw from anything at all. Some of the high-scoring essay writers choose to draw examples from history and literature, but some of them draw examples from their own lives. In fact, the high-scoring essay on page 200 of *The Official SAT Study Guide for the New SAT* uses two personal examples that are almost certainly made up.

SAT Essay Rule 4: Some Imperfect Grammar Is Okay

The high-scoring essays that appear in *The Official SAT Study Guide For The New SAT* are full of mistakes that would qualify as errors for the Identifying Sentence Errors portion of the Writing Section. For example, the high-scoring essay on page 120 of the College Board's book improperly shifts from the present tense to the past tense, uses the word *alright*, and starts a sentence with the conjunction *however*. So you can get away with a few grammatical mistakes and still score a perfect 6.

SAT Essay Rule 5: The Longer, The Better

All the high-scoring sample essays included in *The Official SAT Study Guide For The New SAT* are fairly long and well-developed, while the low-scoring sample essays are much shorter. But be careful—an essay's score seems to correlate with its length, but that doesn't mean that writing garbage just to fill up space is a good idea. What it means is that if you've written a short essay, your chances of scoring high seem to be just about zero.

SAT Essay Rule 6: Vocabulary Isn't That Important

On page 105 of *The Official SAT Study Guide For The New SAT*, the College Board says it looks for a "varied, accurate, and apt vocabulary" in high-scoring essays. But the essays that receive the highest possible scores demonstrate very little in the way of vocabulary skills. The biggest word in the sample high-scoring essay on page 120 is *dumbfounded*, and, as already mentioned, that essay also uses the word *alright*. The other high-scoring essays have similarly unimpressive vocabularies.

SAT Essay Rule 7: No Set Format

The high-scoring essays in *The Official SAT Study Guide For The New SAT* use a variety of formats. Some seem to use variations on the standard five-paragraph essay; all of them use an opening paragraph and a closing paragraph, both of varying lengths.

SAT Essay Rule 8: Details, Details

The high-scoring essays in *The Official SAT Study Guide For The New SAT* all use detailed examples to support their claims.

SAT Essay Writing Process

This process is an effective way to organize your thoughts and write a response that closely imitates known high-scoring essays. Feel free to use it or adapt it to fit the situation—but make sure any adaptations you make are still in line with the rules for the SAT essay in this Guide.

1. Watch the clock from the beginning.

You only have 25 minutes to plan and write an essay. If you kill just 5 minutes day-dreaming or panicking, you've wasted twenty percent of your time! Do NOT let time get away from you here. This is crucial.

2. Develop a one-word response to the question.

Before you can write this essay, you have to know what you're going to be saying. It sounds simplistic, but you need to focus yourself before you can make effective, efficient use of your time.

This one-word answer will often simply be "yes," "no," or "maybe," but it could just as easily be anything else. Remember that there is no correct answer to an essay question—you can't get this step wrong. The point is simply to focus your mind on the point you're trying to make in your essay.

3. Make up three personal experiences that illustrate your position.

Remember that the SAT scorers don't care whether the examples that illustrate your position are real or not. All they care about is whether you can put together ANY example at all that would support your point.

Since you're going to be making up these examples out of thin air, make sure the relationship between the examples and the answer you've chosen to the prompt is CLEAR and DIRECT. Don't invent an example that's only vaguely related to your answer. This is a blank check—come up with something really good. It will make your score higher, and make the rest of your writing easier.

Also, make sure your examples take the form of a story that happened to you. This will make them easier to relate to your reader.

4. Begin your essay with a one-sentence statement of your answer to the prompt.

The SAT scorers aren't big on subtlety. Start your essay with a flat statement of the point you intend to prove. (For examples of top-scoring essays that did this, see pages 123 and 200 of *The Official SAT Study Guide For The New SAT*.) Refer to your one-word answer in Step 2 if you've forgotten what you were trying to say.

5. Write a "Though" sentence to modify your opening sentence.

The second sentence in your essay should start out by contradicting your first sentence with the word *though*, and then finish the sentence with a comma and a re-affirmation of the idea in the first sentence. That might sound a little complicated, so let's try an example. If the first sentence is

The police are a positive and protective force in American society.

then the second sentence is

Though some may criticize the police forces in major cities for being too quick to resort to violence, without the police there would be violence everywhere.

See how that works? The first sentence says *X*. Then the second sentence starts with the word *though* and introduces an idea that contradicts *X*; the second sentence finishes with a comma and then an idea that restates *X*. (The reason for using the word *though* in this way is that it guarantees you'll have a sentence with an interesting structure, something common to all high-scoring essays.)

6. Finish the first paragraph with a sentence that gives a strong introduction to your examples

Make the last sentence in the first paragraph a simple transitional sentence that introduces the two examples you thought of in Step 3. To finish the imaginary first paragraph that we started in Step 6, we might write a sentence like

Three episodes from my personal experience serve as compelling examples of this fact.

See? Nothing too fancy. At this point, you're finished with the first paragraph—the groundwork has been done, and the hardest part of the essay is behind you!

7. Begin the second paragraph with a general statement that introduces your first example.

This first sentence of the second paragraph serves to introduce your first example. Make it something general. See the sample essay on page 200 of the College Board Publication *The Official SAT Study Guide For The New SAT* for an example—there the first sentence of the second paragraph is *Sometimes deception occurs in the form of white lies*, and then the rest of the first paragraph is a (probably made-up) example from the author's life in which deception took the form of a white lie.

8. In 3-5 sentences, tell the story that goes with your first example.

In the middle of the second paragraph you'll insert the story that goes with your first example. Don't draw any lessons or anything at this point—just set the stage and explain what happened. Take your time here—remember that you can't score high if you don't put some detail in your examples.

9. In this first story, say that someone or something was like something else.

This is your chance to use a simile, which is a figure of speech in which you compare two things using the word *like*. For an example, see page 200 of *The Official SAT Study Guide For The New SAT*, where the writer says a dress was a like a bunch of cabbages.

Why do you do this? Because it makes the scorer think you have a good command of the English language.

10. Use a sentence or two to relate the story to the first sentence in the essay.

Now that you've told the story you made up, you need to re-connect it to the first sentence you wrote so you can close out this paragraph and move on. So write one or two sentences in which you point out the lesson you learned from the story—and make sure it really relates to the first sentence in your essay!

11. Repeat steps 7, 8, and 10 for the third paragraph with your second example.

The first example is out of the way. Now you'll just go through the second example in the same way, and that will provide your third paragraph. Notice that we leave out the simile from Step 9 in the second example—this saves time and keeps the essay from looking too formulaic to the reader.

12. Repeat steps 7, 8, and 10 for the fourth paragraph with your third example.

Remember, we're just cranking out paragraphs that illustrate our main point. Don't forget to add the details and relate everything back to the main point at the end.

13. Begin the final paragraph with a sentence that relates all of your examples back to the first sentence in your essay.

At this point you're starting to close the essay, so you want to wrap everything up. The first sentence of your last paragraph is going to put your three examples back into the context of the main point you're trying to make.

14. Finish the essay with a sentence that rephrases the first sentence in the essay.

The last thing that remains is to cap off your essay with a sentence that re-establishes the main point of your essay. Of course, you don't want to use the exact same wording that you used in Step 4, but you do want to make roughly the same point with this sentence that you made in Step 4.

SAT Essay Writing Process Conclusion

Believe it or not, this simple 14-step process will help you crank out winning essays with just a little bit of practice. You'll notice that it doesn't give you much room to be creative, but creativity isn't the point—all we want is a reliable, predictable way to get a top score every time.

You've probably also noticed that this formula is very repetitive—it restates the main point of the essay at least four times. Don't let that bother you. The readers go through your essays so quickly that they won't even notice you banging them over the head with the same point. And besides, as the sample essays in the College Board publication *The Official SAT Study Guide For The New SAT* demonstrate, this is the way the SAT wants you to write its essays anyway.

Using The SAT Essay Writing Process

To prove that the SAT Essay Writing Process works, we'll show it to you in action against the essay question from the first sample test in the College Board publication *The Official SAT Study Guide For The New SAT*, which appears on page 389. We'll also use the College Board's own online essay-scoring service to grade the result.

To show you how made-up your essay examples can be, I've concocted completely ridiculous illustrations. Don't actually be that extreme on test day!

Please note that the essay below contains lots of bad grammar and misused words. I did this to show you the relatively low standards of the SAT Essay.

Sample "Perfect Score" Essay

[The essay response below was written for the prompt on page 389 of the College Board publication *The Official SAT Study Guide For The New SAT*. It was scored with the College Board's automated online essay-scoring service, and received a perfect score.]

Necessity motivates people to change. Though we might like to believe that we change of our own free will to become better human beings, the fact is that the desire to change must come from an outside force. Three personal experiences from my recent time as Chief Counsel of the Zlotga tribe on the planet Meep serve to illustrate this point very clearly.

Some changes are brought about for survival. For instance, the flute-berry pickers of the Zlotga found that flies were infesting their crop. This was a serious threat; the Zlotga depend on their berry harvest for survival, but a sting from one of these flies is like getting hit in the eyeball with a trebuchet. Because it was my duty as Chief Counsel to find solutions to problems, I suggested that the pickers wear gloves. Unfortunately, berry-picking is sacred to the Zlotga and they didn't want gloves to come between their hands and the berries. They continued to pick the berries without gloves, enduring the stings of the flies. Finally, though, the stinging became so painful that the Zlotga could no longer bear it. They had to choose between starving to death and wearing their gloves, and they chose the gloves. The Zlotga changed their sacred ways only in order to stay alive.

Other changes happen because greedy people want to get ahead. When the Zlotga first offered me the position of Chief Counsel, I knew it would mean a big pay raise and a chance to wear the special Flying Robe of Kussel. There was a problem, though. In order to receive the position of Chief Counsel, I had to increase my weight to the traditional seven hundred and seventy-seven pounds. Although it required me to consume tons of berries and lie on the floor for several months, I willingly made this change because it was necessary if I wanted to attain the position of Chief Counsel. I chose to change because my situation required it.

There are still other changes that can be brought about by fashion. Last month, all of Meep was talking about the purple elbow-dye worn by the Vilk, the rival tribe of the Zlotga. This elbow dye was so beautiful that tourists were going to visit the Vilk instead of staying with the Zlotga, and our tribe was losing its tourism money. The tribal leaders asked for my help. I made elbow-dye mandatory for all Zlotga, and also required its use on the knee-caps. This brilliant decision made the Zlotga the most beautiful Meepians of all. Tourists came back to Zlotgaland. They would never have agreed to the change if not for the pressure that was put on them by the Vilk.

Whether we are changing out of a survival necessity, out of personal necessity, or because of a trend, all changes are motivated by a necessity of some sort. People never change unless they have to.

Conclusion

As you can see, the essay portion of the SAT can be beaten fairly easily if we learn to approach it systematically, imitating the high-scoring sample essays provided by the College Board. If you use the approach in this Question-Type Guide in your practice sessions, you'll find you get the hang of it in no time. Good luck!

www.grammatix.com

Grammatix, Inc.

presents

how to attack
SAT
Passage-Based
Reading
like a natural test-taker

This Question-Type Guide will help you improve your performance on Passage-Based Reading Questions. In very little time, you'll learn to use hidden SAT patterns to become a natural test-taker!

General Overview of SAT Passage-Based Reading

My students often tell me that Passage-Based Reading questions are their least favorite questions on the SAT. A lot of people think these questions are too subjective to be part of a standardized test—they think that questions about an author's intentions can be answered in more than one way.

Fortunately, this isn't the case. The answer to an SAT Passage-Based Reading question is every bit as clear and definite as the answer to an SAT Math question. In this Question-Type Guide, I'll show you how natural test-takers identify those answers.

After taking my class, most of my students change their minds about Passage-Based Reading questions. They actually think that the Passage-Based Reading questions are the easiest questions on the entire test, and I tend to agree with them.

Before we can go over the process for these questions, we need to talk about the way the questions are set up. There are basically three kinds of Passage-Based Reading questions:

- Word Use Questions
- Citation Questions
- General Passage Questions

Word Use Questions

These questions ask you how a particular word is used in the passage. They often look like this:

```
In line x, the word "[word]" most nearly means . . .
```

To answer these questions, take the quoted word out of the sentence that's cited in the question, and then substitute each of the answer choices into the cited sentence. Only one of the answer choices will make any sense.

Citation Questions

Citation Questions point you to a specific section of the text and ask you a question about it. They often look like this:

```
The author probably mentions [a particular concept] in line x
in order to . . .
```

To answer a Citation Question, you need to read the cited part of the passage and look for the answer choice that restates most of the citation.

General Passage Questions

These questions ask about the text as a whole. They might look like this:

```
The author of the passage would be most likely to support which
one of the following statements?
```

General Passage Questions are easy to answer once you've answered all the Citation Questions. You just follow the same steps as for Citation Questions, but consider all of the citations in the other questions to be fair game for the General Passage Question.

Notice that none of the question types requires you to read the entire passage. You can read the passage if you want, but it isn't necessary.

The Rules for SAT Passage-Based Reading Questions

Knowing the rules that govern Passage-Based Reading questions will help you answer them.

SAT Passage-Based Reading Rule 1: No More, No Less

The text says exactly what it says—nothing more. For example, if the text says

```
Former presidents make good money giving speeches at
universities.
```

then an answer choice that says

```
Ex-politicians can support themselves as speakers because their
fame makes them popular with young audiences.
```

is probably a wrong answer, because it adds more information than what originally appeared in the text. It may actually be true that ex-politicians are popular with younger audiences, but that isn't what the text says. The text just says that former presidents (not all ex-politicians) make good money giving speeches at universities (not necessarily to younger audiences). The text also doesn't say why this is true, but the wrong answer includes an extra reason (popularity with young audiences).

In other words, you can't read anything at all into the questions or the text. Read the text like a contract, not like a novel. Every word counts, and ONLY the words count.

SAT Passage-Based Reading Rule 2: Objectivity

Although a question might seem like it asks you to speculate about an author's intent, the right answer is actually totally objective. The SAT isn't really asking you what the purpose of a phrase "might" be, even if the test uses that word.

Don't get tricked into thinking that answering a question requires some interpretation on your part. It doesn't. The less you try to interpret what the text says, the more questions you'll answer correctly.

The SAT is designed so that any interpretation at all will quickly become misinterpretation, you'll get questions wrong, you'll lose points, and your score will go down.

SAT Passage-Based Reading Rule 3: One Right Answer

There is one, and only one, correct answer per question. I can't tell you how many times I've heard students complain that some questions have more than one good answer. It isn't true. Every question has one good answer and ONLY one good answer.

You must approach the test with the idea that each question has one right answer, and that you can find this answer with the strategies in this Guide.

The Hidden Patterns of SAT Passage-Based Reading Questions

There are four important hidden patterns in SAT Passage-Based Reading Questions. Learning these patterns makes it easier to find correct answer choices.

Hidden Pattern 1: Word Usage

You can usually expect that every passage on the SAT will have a question about the use of a word in a particular line. The correct answer to the question is ALMOST NEVER the most common meaning of the quoted word. For example, imagine a question like this:

```
In line 63, the word "close" most nearly means
```

```
(A)   near
(B)   similar
(C)   miserly
(D)   quiet
(E)   strong
```

We can be fairly sure that (A) is a wrong answer, since "near" is the most common meaning for the word *close*.

Hidden Pattern 2: Ordered, Relevant Citations

Many of the Passage-Based Reading questions will refer you to a specific part of the text to find the answer for a question. For the most part, the citations will lead you through the text in order. In other words, Citation Questions will usually be ordered so that the questions with early citations come early in the section, and the questions with later citations come later in the section.

Why do we care about this? The ordering of the Citation Questions means that we can use our answers to those questions to gain a good understanding of the passage.

The SAT cites all the important portions of the passage—IN ORDER—so that you don't have to read the passage. You can simply read the citations, which you would have to do anyway in the course of answering the questions. Then, when you go back and do all the General Passage Questions, you can answer them with the information you gained from answering the Citation Questions.

Hidden Pattern 3: Wrong Answers

Like every other question type on the SAT, the Passage-Based Reading Questions have recurring patterns of wrong answers that we can use as clues in our search for the right answer. There are four major types of wrong answers that we'll run into. To demonstrate them, we'll use a fake line of text from an imaginary reading passage, along with four wrong answer choices.

Example Citation:
`. . . Researchers have shown that Benjamin Franklin's sister`
`was visually impaired, which might explain the amount of energy`
`that Franklin invested in the invention of bifocals. . . .`

Example Question:
`According to the citation, research suggests that Benjamin`
`Franklin invented bifocals because`

Wrong Answer Type 1: Extra Information

In this wrong answer we find some information that was mentioned in the citation, and some information that was never mentioned in the citation at all.

    `(A) his sister was having difficulty seeing the equipment that`
        `she used to run her dress shop.`

In this example, the wrong answer adds information about the specific problems that the sister was having with her vision.

Wrong Answer Type 2: Direct Contradiction

This type of wrong answer directly contradicts something in the citation.

    `(B) his sister's perfect vision served as an inspiration.`

Here, the wrong answer choice contradicts the cited fact that the sister has poor vision.

Wrong Answer Type 3: Complete Irrelevance

This type of wrong answer has absolutely nothing to do with the cited text. These wrong answers can actually be very tempting to a lot of students. They can't believe the SAT would offer them an answer choice that's obviously wrong, but that's exactly what the test does.

    `(C) he wanted to be able to read his newspapers without putting`
        `on a different pair of glasses.`

This wrong answer has nothing to do with anything mentioned in the passage.

Wrong Answer Type 4: Confused Concepts

This type of wrong answer uses a lot of the ideas mentioned in the citation, but messes up the relationships between them.

    `(D) his sister invested in a cure for his vision problems.`

This one mentions the sister, the investing, the vision problems, and the idea that the bifocals would correct the problem, but it messes up the relationships between those ideas.

IMPORTANT! Those Wrong Answer Types, or combinations of them, will account for most of the wrong answers for Passage-Based Reading Questions. Basically, they all boil down to the idea that wrong answers provide information that differs from the information found in the citation.

Hidden Pattern 4: Right Answer Pattern

There is only one Right Answer Pattern in the Passage-Based Reading Section. Right answers are often direct restatements of the words and phrases in the citation. Right answers address the question completely. They don't leave anything out, and they don't add any extra information.

    (E) of his sister's difficulty in seeing.

Here, the phrase *difficulty in seeing* is very similar to the phrase *visually impaired* in the citation. Nothing more, nothing less.

This is really the only Right Answer Pattern for Passage-Based Reading Questions. Since there's only one pattern, you can usually find it in the same way, over and over. It gets to be easy!

www.grammatix.com

SAT Passage-Based Reading Process

Now that we've explained the rules and patterns of SAT Passage-Based Reading Questions, let's look at the process you should use to answer these types of questions.

1. Skim the passages as quickly and superficially as you can.

It may sound strange, but the best way to address SAT Critical Reading is to read each passage as little as possible the first time around. (In fact, when possible, you should do your best to skip the reading the entire passage altogether.) There are two main reasons for this. First, reading the passage too closely is either going to bore you to sleep or distract you from your main focus, which should be attacking the SAT in a systematic way, like a machine. Second, reading the passage is mostly a waste of time anyway, because many SAT questions will refer you to specific parts of the passage that you will have to read again later.

Your only goal at this point is to get a rough idea of some of the concepts that appear in the passage. That's all. Once you've done that, you move on to the first question.

2. Identify the type of Passage-Based Reading Question you're dealing with.

```
[If it's a Word Use Question, proceed to Step 3.]
[If it's a Citation Question, proceed to Step 5.]
[If it's a General Passage Question, proceed to Step 10.]
```

3. Find the quoted word in the text.

Remove that word from the sentence in the text, and replace it with each answer choice. Read each new sentence with the substituted word, and see if it makes any sense. One of the new sentences should make a lot more sense than the other four new sentences. The one that makes the most sense is the one you like.

4. Check for hidden SAT patterns.

If the answer you like is also the first thing that comes to mind when you think of the quoted word from the question, reconsider your answer.

```
[If you're absolutely certain that you have the right answer, then
mark that answer on your answer sheet.]

[If you're not absolutely certain, DON'T mark an answer.  If
you're not certain, you'll probably be wrong, and you'll lose
points.  DON'T GUESS!  If you don't remember why you shouldn't
guess, check out our guessing discussion earlier in this Guide.]
```

5. Read the citation.

Find the citation in the text that the question is referring to. Read it. If the citation is a line citation and the cited line picks up in the middle of a sentence, go back up to the beginning of that sentence and start there. (It may also help to read the sentence before or after the citation, but this usually isn't necessary.)

www.grammatix.com

6. Find four wrong answers.

It's important to look for wrong answers first. When you come across an answer that matches one of the wrong answer patterns we talked about, cross it out.

    [If you cross out exactly four answer choices, go to Step 7.]

    [If you cross out all five answer choices, go to Step 8.]

    [If you cross out fewer than four answer choices, go to Step 9.]

7. Look at the remaining answer choice.

See if the remaining answer choice fits the right answer pattern (in other words, see if it restates essential points in the citation). If it does, that's great. If it doesn't really fit any pattern at all, but the other answers are all clearly wrong, you can still be pretty sure you have the right answer.

    [If you're sure that you're right, mark the answer and move on to
    the next question.]

    [If you're not completely sure, DON'T GUESS. If you don't
    remember why you shouldn't guess, look at our guessing discussion
    from earlier in this Guide.]

8. Keep trying.

Believe it or not, crossing out all five answers is actually better than not crossing out enough answers. It means that you're reading with a critical eye, which is exactly the right way to handle the SAT!

Now you have to figure out where you went wrong. Look at the citation and the answer choices again, and see if you can figure out where your mistake is. (If necessary, read the lines immediately before and immediately after the citation.)

    [If you can find your mistake, go back to Step 6.]

    [If you can't find your mistake, and none of the answers look
    good, then skip the question. Don't ever guess. If you don't
    remember why you shouldn't guess, look at our guessing
    discussion.]

9. Be more critical.

You aren't reading the passage critically enough. Remember that it's important to look for wrong answers. If you can find any reason at all not to like an answer choice, cross it out and move on the next choice. If necessary, read the lines immediately before and immediately after the citation.

    [If you can find more wrong answers, go back to Step 6.]

    [If you can't find more wrong answers, skip the questions. Don't
    guess from the answers that you haven't eliminated. You'll
    probably be wrong, and you'll lose points. If you don't remember
    why you shouldn't guess, look at our guessing discussion.]

10. Save General Passage Questions for later.

Skip General Passage Questions until you've answered all the Citation Questions. Once you've answered (or skipped) all the Citation Questions, go back to the General Passage Questions. Go to Step 5, and use ALL the citations in the Citation Questions you've answered to help you answer the General Passage Questions. By the time you've answered all the Citation Questions, you probably won't need to do a whole lot of reading to answer the General Passage Questions. If you do need to do extra reading, remember to keep it as close to skimming as possible—don't waste time and energy immersing yourself in a passage.

Two Important Notes

There are two important things you should keep in mind while answering Passage-Based Reading questions.

1. **Make sure you read questions and citations COMPLETELY.**
   If you miss a word like *not* or *because*, you won't be able to answer the question correctly.

2. **Make sure you read the key parts of the passage.**
   Even if the question doesn't ask you to, it's usually a good idea to read these key parts of the passage:
   - the italicized introduction to the passage
   - the opening sentence of the passage
   - the closing sentence of the passage

These parts of the passage will often contain key information that gives you an idea of the passage, and it only takes a few seconds to read them!

SAT Passage-Based Reading Process Conclusion

That's it!

When you use this process, you're basically looking for reasons NOT to like each answer choice. When you've identified four wrong answer choices, you look for a reason that you like the remaining answer choice!

Now we'll show you this incredible process IN ACTION against real SAT questions!

Using the SAT Passage-Based Reading Process

To prove that our SAT Passage-Based Reading Process works, we'll go through all the Passage-Based Reading Questions in a randomly chosen portion of a real SAT taken from the College Board Publication *The Official SAT Study Guide For the New SAT*.

Question 9, page 391

This is a Citation Question. We find the cited part of the passage and read from the sentence that starts with "Studies show . . ." to the phrase " . . . in a mirror." Now we look for patterns in the answer choices to match the wrong answer patterns we want to find.

(A) is irrelevant to the passage, because nothing in the passage suggests that dolphins are more or less sensitive to their environment than any other animal.

(B) is also irrelevant—nothing in the passage mentions captivity.

(C) contradicts the passage. The passage describes dolphins doing things that we do all the time, which means that these things cannot be "unique" to them.

(D) is irrelevant, just like (A) and (B) were. Nothing in the description suggests that dolphins are especially playful.

(E) is the correct answer choice—all of the skills listed in the passage are skills that humans have.

Since we can see that every choice but (E) follows a wrong answer pattern, and since (E) essentially restates the information from the passage, we mark (E) and go on to the next question.

Question 10, page 391

This is a General Passage Question, because it asks about the general approach of the author of Passage 2. We skip these types of questions and come back to them after all the Citation Questions have been answered. In this case, though, the only Citation Question about these passages is question 9, and we've already answered it.

As always, we'll answer this question without doing too much in-depth reading. We already know that the author of Passage 1 thinks dolphins might be as intelligent as humans. From skimming Passage 2, especially the last sentence of Passage 2, we can see that Passage 2 is more cautious than Passage 1 was about the nature of dolphin intelligence. Passage 2 doesn't say anything definite about how intelligent dolphins are or aren't; it only says that human intelligence and dolphin intelligence are different things. Knowing that, let's look for our answer patterns:

(A) is no good because Passage 2 doesn't say anything about whether it's possible to measure intelligence. That makes this one irrelevant.

(B) is correct because it basically restates the last two sentences of Passage 2, exactly as we would expect an ideal right answer to do.

(C) is irrelevant—Passage 2 doesn't say anything about objectivity.

(D) is also irrelevant. Passage 2 doesn't say anything about whether or not dolphin activities require high intelligence.

(E) is also irrelevant to the passage. Passage 2 doesn't say anything about how much we know about dolphins' social activity.

The SAT likes to give you correct answers that basically restate a relevant part of the passage, and that's just what it's done here.

 IMPORTANT! Even though this question uses subjective language like "would most likely respond," remember that the test NEVER asks you to be subjective. There is always one right answer to each SAT question, and with the right approach you can find it every time.

Question 11, page 391

This is another General Passage Question. In this question, we're being asked to compare our authors' views on dolphin intelligence. Since we've already read or skimmed most of both passages to answer the first two questions, this one shouldn't be too hard.

(A) adds extra information to Passage 1 because it mentions "culture," which doesn't appear anywhere in either passage.

(B) changes the message of Passage 1 slightly. That passage says dolphins "may be" nearly as intelligent as humans, but this answer choice says that they "are as intelligent." So this choice is already incorrect with respect to Passage 1, and we don't even need to consider what it says about Passage 2.

(C) is irrelevant to both passages, because the first author doesn't address the idea of ranking animal intelligence and the second rejects the idea.

(D) is correct because it rephrases key parts of both passages. The last sentence of Passage 1 establishes that the author thinks dolphins are "highly intelligent," and the last sentence of Passage 2 ("until we know more") establishes that its author thinks we don't have enough grounds to make any claims about dolphin intelligence.

(E) is wrong about Passage 1, which never mentions brain size at all.

Question 12, page 391

This is another General Passage question about both passages. We're looking for the statement that's supported by both passages. Since we've just answered three questions about these passages, and the passages are relatively short, we should be able to handle this question without having to do any re-reading. Let's see if it works.

(A) is something that appears in Passage 1 but not Passage 2.

(B) is something that doesn't appear in either passage—we never read anything about emotions.

(C) is another thing that doesn't appear in either passage.

(D) is just about the only thing the two passages seem to agree on. Both authors agree that dolphins have some intelligence—they just disagree on how much or what it's used for.

(E) is wrong because only Passage 1 mentions tool usage.

There we go—that wasn't so bad, was it? On to the next passage!

Question 13, page 392

This is a Citation Question, so we'll go ahead and answer it by using the cited sentence. Let's check out our answer choices:

(A) is wrong because the citation doesn't say anything about a less complicated time.

(B) is wrong because nothing has been said about religion.

(C) contradicts the text, in a way, because the citation points out the similarity between two eras (Native Americans are misunderstood in both), while this answer choice talks about a contrast.

(D) is also incorrect because there's not "myth" mentioned in our citation.

(E) is correct because it restates exactly what the citation does. The citation says that things now are just as they were then with respect to the way people understand Native Americans; the answer choice says that the citation draws a parallel between the old situation and the current situation. This is a model correct answer for an SAT Passage-Based Reading question.

Since we've successfully found four answer choices that fit our wrong answer patterns and one answer choice that fits our right answer pattern, we can mark our choice with certainty and move on to the next question.

Question 14, page 393

This is a Word Use Question. We find the cited sentence, remove the word "charged" from it, and try each answer choice in the sentence to see which one makes sense.

It becomes pretty clear that (D) is the only answer choice that fits in the sentence and makes any real sense. Looking for a wrong answer pattern, we see that (A) is the meaning that probably comes to most people's minds when the think of the word "charged," but it's incorrect here because it doesn't fit the context of the citation.

Question 15, page 393

This is a Citation Question. We read line 14 and use it to answer the question.

(A) is a wrong answer because nothing has been said about philosophy. Be careful here—the SAT wants you to over-think this answer choice and choose it. But remember that, whenever possible, the correct answer shouldn't add anything to the text. If this were the correct answer, it would be injecting the idea of philosophy into the text where it doesn't exist.

(B) is the correct answer because it restates the cited line. Line 14 says the idea is "not new," and mentions Rousseau as an example of an eighteenth-century thinker who also subscribed to the idea. This answer choice restates that by referring to the length of time that a bad idea can survive.

(C) is totally irrelevant to the citation, so it has to be wrong.

(D) is also wrong because there's no mention of European intellectual diversity— never read anything into the citation!

(E) is wrong because this citation doesn't mention anything about the fallibility of great thinkers—it only cites a great thinker in order to establish a period in history when a certain bad idea existed.

Question 16, page 393

For this Citation Question, we'll probably want to read the sentence immediately preceding the cited sentence, since the cited sentence uses the pronoun *it*—we want to see what *it* refers to.

We can see that *it* is the idea that Native Americans were similar to Stone-Age Europeans. We also see, by finishing the sentence that starts on line 28, that this idea is false. With that in mind, let's attack the answer choices:

(A) simply restates the falsehood that's established by the word "difficulty" at the end of the sentence that begins on line 28. Since it restates the relevant part of the text, it's exactly the kind of answer choice we're looking for.

(B) is similar to the wrong answer we might expect to find if this were a simple Word Use Question. A "crowd-pleaser" normally would be some sort of "entertaining novelty," but in this context that phrase doesn't do anything to restate the text.

(C) is incorrect because there's no "deception" being mentioned anywhere in this citation.

(D) is no good for the same reason as (C)—there's no benefit described in the passage.

(E) is also wrong, because no "revolution" is mentioned anywhere.

Yet again, we see several wrong answers that fail to restate the citation in the text, and one correct answer choice that does restate it. We mark (A) and move on.

Question 17, page 393

Notice that we just answered a question about line 28, and this question is about the same sentence. Remember that the Citation Questions on the SAT will typically lead us through the text in order.

Let's look at our answer choices:

(A) is the correct answer because it refers to the idea incorporated in the beginning of the cited sentence—the *it* we talked about in Question 16 is the belief that Native Americans resembled the ancestors of more developed Europeans.

(B) is totally irrelevant—nothing in the passage mentions the consensus of the anthropological community.

(C) is irrelevant because the citation does not mention popular culture at all.

(D) is irrelevant because no such theories appear here.

(E) is an example of a wrong answer that confuses concepts from the passage—the passage mentions misconceptions about Native American communities, not about European ones.

Question 18, page 393

This is another Citation Question, which we'll answer, once again, by reading the cited sentence and then attacking the answer choices.

(A) is irrelevant because the passage doesn't talk about fueling myths.

(B) is also irrelevant, because the passage does not mention conventional logic.

(C) restates end of the cited sentence, which says that the things at the beginning of the sentence were necessary for the Native Americans; otherwise, they would have "vanished long ago." This is exactly the sort of restatement we have come to expect from correct answers to these kinds of SAT questions.

(D) is no good because the cited part of the passage doesn't mention historians at all.

(E) is wrong because this part of the passage doesn't mention anything about cultures influencing each other.

Question 19, page 393

For this Citation Question, we look at lines 52 and 53 and see that they both contain the pronoun *they*, so we read the previous sentence to find out who *they* is referring to. We see that *they* refers to Native Americans, and also that these two sentences are examples of the European beliefs about Native Americans. Now we're ready to look at our answer choices.

(A) is the correct answer; it even reuses the word *perceive*, which appears in the sentence we had to read in order to understand who "they" were in lines 52 and 53.

(B) is irrelevant, as no research is mentioned.

(C) confuses the concepts in the passage, because the cited part of the passage is about the way Europeans thought of Native Americans, not vice-versa.

(D) is also irrelevant; we're not told whether anyone accepted these criticisms.

(E) is completely irrelevant, just like (B) and (D).

Question 20, page 393

After we read lines 66 through 70 for this Citation Question, we're ready to attack the answer choices again. (Note, as usual, that line 66 starts in the middle of a sentence. It isn't a bad idea to read that entire sentence as well—it will only take you another second or two.)

(A) contradicts the citation, which says that Western historians are happy to use archaeological evidence.

(B) restates the main idea of the citation, which is that Western historians are unable to learn anything about Native Americans because their approach to knowledge is too constraining.

(C) is irrelevant, since credentials aren't mentioned in the citation.

(D) is also irrelevant; nothing is mentioned anywhere about whether anyone is well-meaning.

(E) is also totally incorrect—the citation doesn't say anything about anyone's predecessors.

Question 21, page 393

Note that this question puts you right back in the same citation you just read to answer question 20. Remember that the SAT cites these passages in order to make it easier for you to follow them. Let's take a look at the answer choices.

(A) is irrelevant to the cited part of the passage. Also, if you read the beginning of the sentence that starts on 66 to answer the previous question, you'll remember that the educated guess would NOT be based on something numerical or exact, like statistics.

www.grammatix.com

(B) is right for two reasons. First, it's the only answer choice that isn't precluded by the citation for the previous question. Second, it's a direct restatement of the sentence that ends in line 66, which we read for the previous question—these are the exact terms used in lines 64 and 65 of that sentence.

(C) contradicts the citation we've been using for these two questions, which says that archaeological evidence would NOT be an educated guess.

(D) is wrong for the same reason as (C)—it's another example of archaeological evidence.

(E) is just like (C) and (D).

At first glance, you might notice that the correct answer to this question actually comes from something that was cited for the previous question. This might seem to violate the rule about ordered, relevant citations, and the idea that we don't need to read any more than the cited parts of the text to find our answers. Actually, though, it only serves to prove the existence of the rule—what's really going on here is that the SAT can't ask you a question like 21 unless it has already asked you a question like 20.

Question 22, page 393

We have another citation question here, and we begin, as always, by reading the entire sentence that includes the cited lines. Once we've done that, we can attack the answer choices:

(A) can't be the right answer because one of the places listed in the citation is in the United States, so it contradicts the text.

(B) isn't the right answer because, as we've seen, all the arguments in this passage are about the world's misconceptions about Native Americans, not about academic homogenization.

(C) is the right answer because it restates the cited part of the text. The ideas of "every modern observer" and "folklore" in the text match the words *universality* and *notions* in the answer choice, respectively.

(D) is irrelevant to the cited part of the passage because nothing is said about a commonality between Native Americans and anyone else.

(E) contradicts the text, in a way, because the cited part of the text is about a universal agreement on certain misconceptions about Native Americans, not about differences between observers.

Question 23, page 394

To answer this Citation Question, we'll start, as always, by reading the cited part of the text, which is at line 82. Now we consider our answer choices:

(A) is irrelevant to the cited portion of the text, so it has to be wrong.

(B) restates the idea of "abandon[ing] . . . fantasies," which is exactly what we'd expect the right answer to do. This is the correct choice.

(C), like (A), is irrelevant—nothing here seems related to the idea of hopelessness.

(D) is wrong for the same reason (C) and (A) are.

(E) is similar to the other four wrong answers because it is irrelevant to the cited portion of the passage.

Question 24, page 394

This question follows a pattern we've seen already, building on the citation in the previous question. For that reason, we probably don't even need to re-read the cited passage before attacking the answer choices (though you certainly can if you feel like it, of course).

(A) is correct because it restates the idea in the citation. Where the citation talks about how "students" "start," the answer choice talks about "beginning scholars."

(B) is irrelevant because the citation doesn't say anything about university programs.

(C) is irrelevant also—nowhere in the citation does the author mention progressive scholars.

(D) doesn't present any ideas that appear in the citation, so it's irrelevant and wrong too.

(E) is completely irrelevant as well. The idea of funding doesn't appear anywhere in the citation.

Conclusion

If you've read, studied, and understood everything in this Strategy Guide, you should be able to answer Passage-Based Reading Questions with almost perfect accuracy! We've talked about the rules for these questions, the patterns you can find in the questions, and the process you should use to answer them. We also applied the SAT Passage-Based Reading Process to real SAT Questions from the College Board Publication *The Official SAT Study Guide For the New SAT* so you could see the process in action.

 The most important thing to remember about answering SAT Passage-Based Reading Questions is that EVERY WORD of the right answer has to be right. That's why it's often easier to find the four wrong answers before you look for the right one!

Now that we have SAT Passage-Based Reading under our belts, let's take a look at SAT Sentence Completion!

www.grammatix.com

Page 41

Grammatix, Inc.

presents

how to attack

SAT

Sentence

Completion

like a natural test-taker

This Strategy Guide will help you improve your performance on Sentence Completion Questions. In very little time, you'll learn to use hidden SAT patterns and your knowledge of English to become a natural test-taker!

www.grammatix.com

General Overview of SAT Sentence Completion

Students tend to think that Sentence Completion Questions are relatively easy. It's great that they can feel confident when it comes to these questions. But it's also important not to take these questions lightly—it's easy to make mistakes on this section, and those mistakes will cost you points!

In this Strategy Guide, we'll go over the ways that natural test-takers find the answers to Sentence Completion Questions. But before we can do that, we need to talk about the format of these questions.

There are two types of Sentence Completion Questions, and they're very similar to each other. The first type is the Single-Blank Question, and the second is the Double-Blank Question. The only difference between them is that the first type asks you to fill in one blank, and the second type asks you to fill in two blanks. You use basically the same process to answer either question type.

Most students try to approach SAT Sentence Completion questions by memorizing hundreds or thousands of vocabulary entries. This is a terrible idea, leftover from the days when the SAT had analogies and antonyms on it (but even then, memorization was a bad idea).

Even though there's a whole industry built around teaching SAT vocabulary to high school students, there are a lot of problems with cramming vocab in order to raise your SAT score. For one thing, the vast majority of the words you'll study will never appear on test day, which makes cramming very inefficient. On top of that, the vocabulary words you *do* see on test day will almost never be used in the sense you memorized, so all your cramming may just end up confusing you.

But the biggest reason not to cram is that everyone, no matter how advanced their vocabulary, eventually comes to an unknown word on the SAT. When that happens to natural test-takers, they know the techniques to find solutions without relying on the meanings of every single word in the question. And once you know how to answer questions without knowing all the words, why not use those techniques all the time? So the biggest problem with cramming is that it keeps you from focusing on techniques that are easier, faster, and more efficient.

Let's start learning those new techniques now!

The Rules for SAT Sentence Completion Questions

Knowing the rules of Sentence Completion questions is essential to answering them correctly!

SAT Sentence Completion Rule 1: Key Words

Words like *not, unlike, although, because,* and *while* are used to show relationships between key ideas in the sentences. For example, if we have a sentence like

> Even though her opponent won their first debate, Sally was
> _____ about her chances to win the race.

then we can use the phrase *even though* to figure out that the word in the blank should mean something that goes AGAINST the idea of Sally's opponent winning their first debate. In this case, we might expect the answer to be a word like *hopeful* or *optimistic*.

SAT Sentence Completion Rule 2: Restate the Question

Wherever possible, the correct answer choice must restate part of the prompt sentence. If we have a sentence like

> The computer hardware is designed to be _____ : every
> system is supported by a similar system that performs the same
> function.

then we aren't merely looking for a word that will complete the sentence in a rational way— we're looking for a word that actually means something like "every system was supported by a similar system that performed the same function." For example, a word like *effective* would be an "okay" word to complete the sentence:

> The computer hardware is designed to be effective: every system
> is supported by a similar system that performs the same
> function.

But that doesn't really feel solid. *Effective* goes along with the idea of the sentence, but it doesn't specifically address the idea of similar systems that perform the same function. A much better choice would be a word like *redundant*.

> The computer hardware is designed to be redundant: every system
> is supported by a similar system that performs the same
> function.

Redundant doesn't just "go along with" the idea in the sentence. It actually means "supported by a similar system that performs the same function." Whenever we can, we want to choose words that are restatements of the key phrases in the prompt sentence.

---

www.grammatix.com

SAT Sentence Completion Rule 3: The Perfect Fit

In Double-Blank Sentence Completion Questions, both words MUST fit perfectly in their blanks. A lot of students answer Double-Blank Questions by finding a good fit for only one of the blanks in the question but not the other. That's no good! You have to treat each blank as though it were the only blank in a Single-Blank Question.

These three rules serve as the foundation for the patterns and strategies that natural test-takers use on Sentence Completion questions. In the next section, we'll take a look at those patterns and explain the strategies that come from them.

The Hidden Patterns of SAT Sentence Completion Questions

The patterns that we find in SAT Sentence Completion questions have to do with the types of wrong and right answers that appear in them.

Hidden Pattern 1: Opposites

Very often, we can find wrong answer choices that are the opposite of the correct answer choice. If we have a sentence like the one above about Sally, where the correct answer choice is a word like *optimistic*, then we might expect a wrong answer choice like *despondent*.

Hidden Pattern 2: Similarities

Sometimes we can find a wrong answer that "looks like" the right answer. To use the same example about Sally, if the right answer choice is *optimistic*, then we might see a wrong answer like *optimal*—a word that sounds a little like the right word, but has a completely different meaning.

Hidden Pattern 3: Same Subject, Wrong Answer

There will often be a wrong answer that has something vaguely in common with the concepts in the prompt sentence, but does not fit in the sentence at all. It's important to be on the lookout for these!

Hidden Pattern 4: Say That Again

The right answer will very often be a restatement of something in the prompt sentence, as we saw above in the example with *redundant*.

Special Sentence Completion Techniques: Using the Happy/Sad Test with Context Clues, Prefixes, and Cognates

Like we said in the General Overview, when it comes to Sentence Completion Questions, the goal of the Grammatix SAT Method is to find correct answers without cramming vocabulary. (Just to refresh your memory, cramming vocab is a bad idea because, among other things, you'll be wasting most of your cramming time with words that will never appear on the test, and the words that *do* appear on the test are very rarely used in the sense that you memorized.)

To avoid needless cramming, we'll need to use three Special Techniques:

- Using The Happy/Sad Test with Context Clues
- Finding Prefixes
- Finding Cognates

Using The Happy/Sad Test With Context Clues

In order to do well on the SAT Sentence Completion Questions, you need to be able to tell which ideas in a sentence go together, and to group similar words together—even when you don't know exactly what the words mean.

When you figure out which ideas in the sentence go together, look for words like *unlike*, *because*, *instead of*, *after*, and *not*. You're just looking for context clues in the prompt sentences, as you would if you were doing any other kind of reading and came across a word you didn't know. Classifying words might be a little harder, since it's a newer skill.

To classify words in the Sentence Completion Questions, we'll use something called the Happy/Sad Test.

The Happy/Sad Test works on the assumption that you speak English. If you speak English, then you have a subconscious knowledge of certain rules and patterns in that language. One of the subconscious things that you know about English is whether a word is "happy" or "sad." If a word is "happy," then it has a positive connotation. If it's "sad," then it has a negative connotation.

To figure out whether a word is happy or sad, all you have to do is listen to the word in your head and notice your first reaction to it. If your first reaction is good, then it's probably a happy word. If it's bad, then you're probably looking at a sad word.

For example, take a word like *lummox*. *Lummox* sounds, to most people, like a "sad" word, even if they don't know what it means. On the other hand, a word like *jollity* sounds "happy," even if you don't know exactly what it means. The Happy/Sad Test doesn't tell us what a word means, but it often tells us whether the word is POSITIVE or NEGATIVE.

www.grammatix.com

When we combine the results of the Happy/Sad Test with our context clues, we can usually figure out whether a blank needs a happy word or a sad word, and which answer choices seem like they have the right connotation to fill that blank.

This can be a very effective technique, as we'll see when we use the SAT Sentence Completion Process.

Sometimes, when students use the Happy/Sad test, they'll incorrectly identify a word as "happy" when it's really negative, or "sad" when it's really positive. THIS IS NOT A PROBLEM. If your idea of a word's happiness or sadness isn't correct, your idea of the happiness or sadness of other words will probably also be wrong—and things will often still work out fine, because the important thing is to be able to group words together. As long as the right words are associated with each other, it doesn't matter if you mislabel the group as a whole.

Natural test-takers use processes like these—based on the way a word *feels*, not on its actual definition—to find the answers to Sentence Completion questions. Natural test-takers use these processes to arrive at answers with certainty, not as a foundation for some useless guessing trick!

Finding Prefixes

As you probably remember from grade school, prefixes are useful for helping you figure out what words might mean. Your teachers probably taught you that *sub-* means "under," *un-* means "the opposite of," et cetera.

But your teachers weren't exactly telling you the whole truth . . .

Those basic meanings for prefixes are usually accurate for basic words, like the ones you learned in elementary school. For example, the *un-* in the word *unforgettable* really does make that word the opposite of the word *forgettable*, just like your teachers said it would. And the *re-* in *reuse* really does show you that you're doing something again, just like we would expect. But remember—these are basic words. You probably already know a basic word like *reuse*, so it doesn't do you much good to be able to take it apart by finding prefixes.

But not all words use prefixes the way we might think, and not everything that we think is a prefix really is one.

For example, the word *understand* is not the opposite of a word like *derstand*, and the word *reason* doesn't mean "to ason again." See the problem? We have to be able to tell when something really and truly *is* a prefix, or we'll get ourselves into trouble.

When it comes to more difficult words, we simply can't expect that all prefixes will work the way we might have learned back in grammar school. So we're going to group SAT Sentence Completion prefixes into three main types:

- Strengthening Prefixes
- Weakening Prefixes
- Directional Prefixes

Strengthening Prefixes

These are prefixes that seem to make a word stronger or more forceful in some way. For example, the *ex-* prefix in the word *exterminate* seems to make it more powerful than just the word *terminate*.

(Note to people with strong vocabularies: I realize that this explanation kind of muddles the history of the word *exterminate*. But for the purposes of answering SAT Questions, we don't care what the word's actual history is—we only care about the perceived effect of each component of the word, because that's what we'll base our answers on if we don't know a word.)

Weakening Prefixes

Weakening prefixes are ones that make a word seem weaker. The prefix *ex-* in the word *ex-president*, for example, serves to weaken the idea of being president—the ex-president isn't the president as much as he used to be.

Directional Prefixes

These are prefixes that give some idea of motion or position. For example, the *ex-* in *external* gives us the idea of being located outside of something.

IMPORTANT! Note that we just used the same prefix in three different senses! I deliberately chose those examples to demonstrate that classifying prefixes is often a matter of following your gut, just like the Happy/Sad Test. Just rely on your "subconscious" knowledge of English, and it will come naturally with practice.

Finding Cognates

For our purposes, two words are cognates if they share similar structures and meanings. For example, the noun *sublimation* and the adjective *sublime* could be considered cognates—if you saw the word *sublimation* on the SAT and didn't know it, you might be able to think of the word *sublime* and get a good enough idea of *sublimation* to be able to answer the question.

It often becomes easier to look for cognates when we've already taken prefixes into account. For example, you might not know the word *parity* if you saw it on the SAT. But you might recognize that it sounds similar to part of the word *disparity*, which comes up often in political discussion or on the news. So, how can you use this information? Well, if you remember the meaning of the word *disparity*, and you can identify *dis-* as a weakening prefix in this case, then you can know that *parity* is the opposite of *disparity*. Or let's say you don't remember the exact meaning of the word *disparity*, but you can tell it sounds "sad" when you use the Happy/Sad Test. If you figure that *dis-* is a weakening prefix, and that *disparity* sounds "sad," then you can be pretty sure that *parity* is "happy." This, in turn, will usually be enough to answer the question.

You can make cognate pairs out of two English words, like in the *disparity/parity* example above, or you can use words from other languages to help you figure out SAT words.

www.grammatix.com

For example, you might not know the word *corpulent*, but you could use the French word *corps* to figure out that *corpulent* has something to do with the body.

IMPORTANT! Looking for foreign-language cognates isn't always easy, and not everyone can do it successfully. Among other things, it depends on which languages you've studied and how well you remember them. So if this particular technique doesn't work terrifically well for you, don't push it—just focus on English-language cognates.

If all of these techniques sound like a lot to master, don't worry. You'll rarely use all of them on the same question, and you'll find that after you've worked with them a little bit they become second nature.

Speaking of that, let's get started on learning the process that pulls all of these techniques together.

SAT Sentence Completion Process

Now that we've explained the rules and patterns of SAT Sentence Completion questions, let's look at the process that I recommend for these types of questions.

1. Identify the type of Sentence Completion Question that you're dealing with.

    [If it's a Single-Blank question, proceed to Step 2.]

    [If it's a Double-Blank question, proceed to Step 5.]

2. Identify the words you don't know.

    [If you know all the words in the answer choices, proceed to Step 3.]

    [If there is only one word in an answer choice that you don't know, proceed to Step 10.]

    [If there are two or more words in the answer choices that you don't know, proceed to Step 11.]

3. Read the prompt sentence to yourself five times.

Every time you read the sentence, replace the blank with another answer choice. If you really know all the words involved, then four answer choices will make no sense and one answer choice will make perfect sense. The one that makes sense is the one you like.

    [If exactly one answer choice makes perfect sense, proceed to Step 4.]

    [Otherwise, go back to Step 2 and make a new choice, because you don't know all the words.]

4. Look for hidden patterns in the answer choices.

Look for answers that are the opposite of the one you like, that are similar to the one you like, and that are kind of similar to the subject matter in the question. If you find them, you can be even more sure that you have the right answer. If you don't find them, it's no big deal—as long as you're still certain that your answer choice is the only answer that makes any sense at all. Look for the choice that you like to restate something in the sentence.

Again, if the pattern is there, you can be even more certain that you have the right answer. If the pattern isn't there, AND if no other choices are restatements of anything in the sentence, then you're still okay.

    [If everything checks out, you can be reasonably certain you have the right answer. Mark your answer and proceed to the next question.]

    [If you aren't certain of the answer, you probably don't know all the words. Go back to Step 2.]

5. Identify the words you don't know.

    [If you know all the words in the answer choices, proceed to Step 6.]

    [If there is only one word in an answer choice that you don't know, proceed to Step 10.]

[If there are two or more words in the answer choices that you don't know, proceed to Step 11.]

6. Choose one of the blanks to focus on first.

Using your knowledge of the prompt sentence and the words in the answer choices, you want to pick the blank that seems to have the FEWEST number of potential correct answers in the answer choices. If you pick wrong, it's no big deal. It's just that it's easier to start with the blank that will take the least amount of effort to show results.

7. Read through the sentence five times.

Every time you read the sentence, substitute a different answer choice in the blank that you chose in Step 5. Because it's a Double-Blank question, there might be more than one answer choice with a decent word for the blank that you focus on first. That's okay. Note the answer choices that seem to fit the blank you started with.

8. Look at the answer choices that you chose in Step 7.

Read the prompt sentence and substitute the other words from those answer choices into the blank that you didn't focus on originally. One of the answer choices should match both blanks and make perfect sense. That's the one that you like.

[If exactly one answer choice makes perfect sense, proceed to Step 9.]

[Otherwise, go back to Step 5 and make a new choice, because you don't know all the words.]

9. Look for hidden patterns that relate to the answer choice you like.

Look for wrong answer patterns in the answer choices that you don't like. If you find them, you can be even more sure that you have the right answer. If you don't find them, it's no big deal (as long as you're still certain that the answer choice you like is the only one that makes any sense at all).

Look for the choice that you like to restate something in the sentence. Again, if the pattern is there, you can be even more certain that you have the right answer. If the pattern isn't there, that's okay—as long as none of the other choices is a restatement of the sentence.

[If everything checks out, you can be reasonably certain you have the right answer. Mark your answer and proceed to the next question.]

[If you aren't certain of the answer, you probably don't know all the words. Go back to Step 5.]

10. Use the Special SAT Sentence Completion Techniques.

Use the special techniques that we talked about to try to get a rough idea of the role of the unknown word—try the Happy/Sad Test, look for cognates, and use context clues. After you've done that, look for relationships to help you figure out the word you don't know. Whether you can figure out the word or not, follow the same processes described in Steps 3 and 6 (depending on whether your question is a single- or double-blank question) to try to answer the question. If you don't know one of the answer choices, skip it. If you find hidden patterns that point to wrong answers in the four answer choices that you know, then the right answer might be the choice you don't know. If you find three answer choices with hidden patterns that point to wrong answers, and if one answer choice has a hidden pattern that points to the right answer, then you can be pretty sure that the choice with the good pattern is right.

> [If you go through the steps above and you're completely certain of your answer choice, mark the answer.]

> [If you're not completely certain, skip the question. DON'T GUESS! If you don't remember why guessing is never a good idea, go back and look at our discussion on guessing.]

11. Use the same Special Techniques described in Step 10.

Look for relationships to help you figure out the words you don't know. Go back to Step 2 and try the process on all the words you know. If you've done everything you can possibly do and you still don't know most of the words, you can only earn the right to mark an answer if you're absolutely certain that one of the words you know is a restatement of the right part of the sentence.

> [If you're completely certain of your answer, mark it.]

> [If you're anything less than certain, skip the question. NEVER, EVER GUESS! If you're not sure why you shouldn't guess, go back and look at our discussion on guessing.]

SAT Sentence Completion Process Conclusion

We've now seen the entire SAT Sentence Completion Process, which lets us figure out answers even when we don't know all the words in the question. The most important part of the process is to make sure, one way or another, that you're completely certain of every answer choice you mark.

The processes that we use to answer SAT Sentence Completion Questions, or any other type of SAT question, are flexible. The process that we've explored in this section should help shape the process that you use on the test, but you may feel free to adjust it as necessary.

The only thing that you have to be absolutely sure of is that you DON'T GUESS!

Using the SAT Sentence Completion Process

To prove that the SAT Sentence Completion Process works, we'll go through some Sentence Completion Questions in a real SAT taken from the College Board publication *The Official SAT Study Guide For the New SAT.*

IMPORTANT!

Remember that you should use *only* real test questions provided by the test-writing company itself whenever possible. That's why Grammatix doesn't write its own fake sample tests—we want you to see that our step-by-step strategies work on real, actual SAT questions from the real, actual SAT.

To show that we don't need to know all the words on the SAT, we'll sometimes proceed as though we don't know some of the words in the question.

Question 1, page 390

We probably know all the words in this question, and it's a single-blank question. While any of the answer choices might make sense if we don't read too closely, only one of them follows Hidden Pattern 4—only one of them restates key phrases in the prompt. (D) restates the phrase "stage scenery" and is also a one-word description of the phrase set off in dashes in the question.

As for wrong answer choices, (A), (B), (C), and (E) all follow Hidden Pattern 3, because they all represent ideas related to the concepts in the prompt.

Question 2, page 390

We might not know either word in choice (C).

This is a double-blank question. Let's start with the first blank, since we have to start somewhere.

Choices (A) and (B) both have options for the first blank that seem like they might restate the idea of "affluence" that appears in the prompt, making them attractive answer choices because of Hidden Pattern 4. Choice (D), on the other hand, has a first-blank word that is the opposite of the idea of "affluence," which means that (D) is likely a wrong answer because it follows Hidden Pattern 1.

Since we like choices (A) and (B) for the first blank, let's take a look at the words those choices have in the second blank. The second blank for choice (A) doesn't really make any sense. A disease can't just "adapt;" the sentence would sound a lot better if it had the diseases adapting TO something, but there's nothing after the blank. So choice (A) breaks Rule 3, because both words don't fit perfectly in their blanks—only the first word in (A) fits perfectly. The second word in choice (B), on the other hand, does fit perfectly. So it looks like (B) is our winner!

Let's check the other answer choices, just to make sure we still like (B) the best. We've already discussed what's wrong with (A) and (D). (E) presents a good choice for the second blank, but the first blank doesn't fit well because "commonness" doesn't restate any part of the prompt—if we had started out by looking at the second blank, we might have liked (E) at first, but we would still see that it violates Rule 3 because of the first blank.

Now, what about (C)—the answer choice with words we might not know? Can we go ahead and mark (B) without knowing the words in (C), or would that be guessing? Well, we know that (B) fits perfectly, and we know that there is always exactly one perfect answer to each question. So in this situation, we're free to mark (B)—no matter what the words in choice (C) mean, they can't possibly be better than (B).

 This is NOT guessing! It's just smart, natural test-taking. Always remember that there is a difference between guessing and operating without complete knowledge of the question. Guessing is marking an answer choice when you aren't certain that it's correct. But by using the rules, patterns, and processes described above, you can arrive at the right answer with certainty even though your knowledge of all the ideas in the question is incomplete—this is what natural test-takers do all the time.

Question 3, page 390

Let's say we have problems with the words in choices (A) and (B).

This is a single-blank question, so let's just try all the words we know in the blank and see what happens.

Note that the key idea here is that people "suffering from various ailments" come to the spring because of the idea in the blank. So we want a choice that fits with the idea of being attractive to people who are suffering. (E) is the choice that restates that idea.

(C) and (D) are both irrelevant to the ideas in the prompt, so we know they're wrong. But what about (A) and (B)? Just like in the last question, even though we don't know what these two words mean, we DO know that one choice fits perfectly—which means that (A) and (B) can't be correct, according to the rules of the SAT. So we can mark (E) with certainty.

Question 4, page 390

For this question, we might not know the first word in choice (A) or the second word in choice (B).

This is a double-blank question. Let's start with the first blank, just for fun.

The key idea here is that the new research is better than anything that came before it. Since that's the case, what has the new research probably done to all the subsequent work in the field? The answer to this question will be the word that goes in the first blank.

The only answer choice that seems to fit nicely in the sentence is (C)—the new work provides a basis for future work. Note that none of the other answer choices fits smoothly in the blank. For example, it doesn't make much sense to say that you "prepared a basis," does it? In everyday English, we don't usually put those words together that way. Remember that every word has to fit perfectly in its blank!

Let's see if the second word for answer choice (C) fits in its blank. Does it make sense to talk about "subsequent investigations?" It sure does—that fits perfectly. So (C) looks pretty good.

Note that (A) and (D) also look good for the second blank, but we've already established that they're bad choices for the first blank, so they can't be correct.

What about our unknown words? Well, does the Happy/Sad test tell us anything? We can probably tell that both the unknown words sound "sad," and it doesn't look like either of those blanks call for sad words.

www.grammatix.com

So the answer is (C)! Let's mark it and move on.

Question 5, page 390

In this question, we probably know all the words in the answer choices.

This is a single-blank question, so we can dive right in and try all the answer choices in the blank.

Remember that we're looking for something that wind can do that will "delay the launch."

The only answer choice that works is (A). Notice that none of the other choices really fits in to the sentence—for example, winds can't "forfeit" or "redouble;" only people can.

This one was relatively straightforward. On to the next!

Question 6, page 390

For this one, we might not know what either word in choice (B) means, or the second word in (D) means.

This is a double-blank question. Since we know more of the words for the first blank, let's start there.

Remember, as always, that we want to identify the key words in the prompt. The prompt says that the word in the first blank must be something that would offend people. Well, that knocks (A), (C), and (E) out of the running—those all follow Hidden Pattern 1, because they give us choices that are the opposite of what we would want.

That means we're stuck dealing with the words we didn't know! But don't worry, we still have a few tricks up our sleeves.

Let's try the second word in (D), since we know the first word in (D) fits well. We might not know what the word *conciliatory* means, but let's put it to the Happy/Sad test. To most people it probably sounds either Happy or sort of neutral. Does that go with what we want in the second blank? Not really—we'd much rather have a Sad word for that second blank, since the prompt is all about how the remarks were offensive. You might also notice that *conciliatory* looks a little bit like *reconcile*, which is a Happy sort of word. This doesn't seem to be a good fit, at least at this stage.

So let's take a look at (B). Both the words in (B) probably seem Sad. As a matter of fact, they both seem pretty harsh, even if you don't know their meanings.

That leaves us with one pair of words that we're pretty sure are both negative, and one pair of words that has one negative word and one word that's probably positive. We know that we need two negative words, so it looks like (B) is our answer! Let's mark it and move on.

www.grammatix.com

Remember, this isn't guessing! We don't know what the words in (B) mean, but we know that all the other choices are bad, and (B) seems to have a very strong likelihood of being correct. This is the natural approach to test-taking.

Question 7, page 390

For this one, we probably know all the words except (E).

This is a single-blank question, so we'll just try the words we know and hope for the best.

Remember that we want a word that restates part of the sentence wherever possible. For this question, we want a word that restates the idea of walking slowly, with a limp.

The only word that does that is (A), which makes (A) our best candidate for the right answer so far.

Let's look at the other choices to see what we have. (C) might be attractive to some people, but you have to be careful here. Remember that we want a word that restates part of the prompt, and nothing in the prompt necessarily indicates that Chris is limping at a "onstant" pace.

What about (E)? Students who've had French or Spanish might recognize this one right away, but let's see what we can figure out using only English cognates. The word seems similar to the words *facility* and *facilitate*. Can we think of anything about those words that would seem to lend itself well to the current situation? Not really.

So it looks like (A) is the winner here. It fits the right answer pattern of restating part of the prompt, and none of the other choices seem to do that at all. On to the next question.

Question 8, page 390

Let's assume that we don't know the meanings of any of the words in the answer choices.

This is a single-blank question.

Ordinarily, we would read through the sentence and substitute the various words in the blank until we found one we liked. That isn't possible here, since we don't know any of the words. So what can we do? Let's try our special techniques.

We'll use the Happy/Sad test first. From the context clues like *melodrama*, *tense*, *emphasize*, and *raising their voices*, we get the idea that we're looking for a "sad" word to go in the blank.

We'll probably decide that (A), (B), and (D) look like they might be "sad." Does that get us anywhere? Well, not really. Let's try something else.

What about cognates? We might come up with any of these cognates:

(A) This word sounds like *emperor*, *imperial*, or *imperative*.

(B) The *in-* looks like it might be a prefix. Where does that leave us with cognates for the root? We might find *scrutiny*, *scrutinize*, *scrupulous*, or even *screw*, if we're grasping at straws.

(C) If we use foreign languages, we might think that this one means something like "living together." If not, we'll probably come up with *vivid* or *vivacious*.

(D) For this one we might come up with *history* or *hysterical*.

(E) This word might make us think of *solicitor* or *soliciting*.

We still haven't gotten very far, and we're running out of techniques! But don't worry. This is just good, old-fashioned problem-solving, and it's what natural test-takers do all the time. It's just that this question might take a little more effort than most, that's all.

Let's go back and take a look at the choices we decided were "sad." We'll use our newly discovered cognates and see if they seem like they might be relevant to the prompt.

(A) doesn't look too good. We usually think of "emperors" as being strong, demanding people—they might raise their voices, but they'd never swoon.

(B) doesn't seem like a good idea either. None of those cognates we thought of seem like they have anything to do the prompt.

(D) seems to be the only answer choice with anything at all going for it. It seems to be "sad," which is good, and at least the cognate *hysterical*, with its idea of excessive emotion, ties into all the key words in the prompt.

Maybe now we're getting somewhere. Suddenly (D) seems like the best fit—we may not know what it means, but two of our special techniques have indicated it might be right, which is more than we can say for any other answer choice. So we'll mark (D) and move on.

A lot of the students reading this will protest that we just guessed to solve this question. But that's not true! This isn't guessing—as I keep saying, this is just using special techniques to analyze a problem and determine the solution. So what if we answered this question without knowing what the words meant? We're still certain that (A), (B), (C), and (E) are no good, and we can see a possible connection between (D) and the prompt.

This might feel like a strange, unreliable way of answering SAT questions. If it seems that way to you, it means you're still thinking as a traditional, cramming-oriented test-taker. Just loosen up a little bit and try using these techniques in practice. After a few questions they'll begin to feel totally natural. Trust me.

Conclusion

This Question-Type Guide has discussed all the rules, patterns, and strategies for SAT Sentence Completion Questions. We've learned a process to answer those questions, and we've used that process on some real SAT questions from the College Board Publication *The Official SAT Study Guide For the New SAT.*

 The most important part of the SAT Sentence Completion Process is that we don't give up just because we don't know a word—but we never guess, either! We rely on the way words feel, and we ALWAYS find four wrong answers and one possible right answer.

Working with this Question-Type Guide and your copy of *The Official SAT Study Guide For the New SAT* will help you get better and better at SAT Sentence Completion questions. Keep it up!

Now we've seen how to handle all SAT Critical Reading Questions. Next we'll take a look at the SAT Math Guide.

www.grammatix.com

Grammatix, Inc.

presents

how to attack

SAT

Math

like a natural test-taker

This Strategy Guide will help you improve your performance on the SAT Math section. You'll learn to use hidden SAT patterns, NOT tedious calculations, to approach the test like a natural test-taker!

www.grammatix.com

General Overview of SAT Math

The Math Questions on the SAT are a very mixed bag. The current version of the SAT features several different types of math; almost everything you could study in high school math is on there except calculus and trigonometry. On top of that, an individual question can be a combination of any of those areas, which makes the questions hard to classify.

Some students cover all the basics of SAT math before they reach high school, and some students take Geometry as seniors and never even have classes in Algebra. For the first type of student, SAT math concepts are almost forgotten; for the second type of student, they are just barely familiar.

 In short, nobody I've ever met has felt completely comfortable with all the math on the SAT. I teach these classes for a living, I can answer every single question in *The Official SAT Study Guide For the New SAT*, and I still don't feel like I know a lot of math. I don't let it bother me, and neither should you!

But that's not all—mastering the key mathematical concepts that can appear on the SAT still won't guarantee a high score. In fact, you probably know some students who are "math geniuses" who still don't make perfect scores on the SAT Math section. You might even be one of those students yourself.

For those students—and for most students, actually—there's something missing when it comes to SAT Math. There's a key idea that they haven't realized yet.

What idea is that? It's the idea that the SAT Math test is NOT a math test, at least not in the sense that you're probably used to. The SAT Math section has very little to do with actual mathematical knowledge. Think of it as a logic test, or a bunch of problem-solving exercises. Actually, the better you get at SAT Math, the more you'll come to realize it's just a game—and the more you come to see it as a game, the better you'll get at it.

The truth is that the SAT Math section is a test of definitions and properties. The calculations themselves aren't complicated, as you'll see when we go through some real test questions. The SAT could have made the calculations difficult, but the calculations themselves are always fairly easy, even on so-called "hard" questions. The only thing that makes SAT Math questions difficult is setting them up.

Natural test-takers do better on the "Math" section because they focus on setting problems up. Most students spend too much time trying to find complicated solutions to the problems on the test. This is very frustrating, and results in very low scores. It's like trying to cook an omelet with a hammer.

Studying this Strategy Guide will help you use the techniques that natural test-takers use to score well on SAT Math. More importantly, this guide will help you come to see the SAT "Math" test for what it really is: a logic test!

Math Concept Review: Building the SAT Math Toolbox

In a moment, we'll talk about how to attack the SAT Math section from a strategic perspective. But first, it's important to make sure we know all the mathematical concepts the SAT is allowed to test (don't worry, there aren't that many of them).

- If you already know all the concepts below, then you don't need to go over them again. Instead, go to the next section and start learning how to attack the test.

- If you're not familiar with some of the concepts below, then take a few minutes to refresh yourself on them.

This concept review is designed to be as quick and painless as possible. If you feel that you'd like a little more of an explanation, the best thing to do is find somebody who's good at math (a teacher, parent, or friend) and ask them to spend a little time explaining things to you.

This concept review might seem easier to you than the actual SAT Math section. That's because the difficulty in SAT Math really comes from the setup of each problem, not from the concepts that the problem involves.

understanding
familiarity

For SAT Math, it's not that important to have a *thorough* of the underlying concepts. All you need is a quick, general with a few basic ideas. So that's all we'll spend time on.

Please note that the toolbox is similar in some ways to chapters 14 through 18 of the College Board publication *The Official SAT Study Guide for the New SAT*, but the toolbox is organized a little differently and presents the material in more discrete units. In addition, the toolbox explains things in plainer language and omits some concepts that are redundant, making it easier to study.

As you're going through this toolbox, you may see concepts that aren't familiar. Before you let yourself get confused, make sure you've read the toolbox through TWICE. You'll probably find that a lot of your confusion clears itself up on the second reading.

www.grammatix.com
Page 63

Properties of integers

- An integer is any number that can be expressed without a fraction, decimal, percentage sign, or symbol.
- Integers can be negative or positive.
- Zero is an integer.
    - Examples: These numbers are integers: -99, -6, 0, 25, 8, 675
                    These numbers are NOT integers: pi, *i*, 96.73, 3/4

- There are even integers and there are odd integers.
- Only integers can be odd or even—a fraction or symbolic number is neither odd nor even.
    - Integers that are even can be divided by 2 without having anything left over.
    - Integers that are odd have a remainder of 1 when they're divided by 2.
    - Examples: These are even integers: -6, 0, 8
                    These are odd integers: -99, 25, 675

- An even number plus an even number gives an even result.
- An odd number plus an odd number gives an even result.
- An odd number plus an even number gives an odd result.
- An even number times an even number gives an even result.
- An even number times an odd number gives an even result.
- An odd number times an odd number gives an odd result.
- Some integers have special properties when it comes to addition and multiplication:
- Multiplying any number by 1 leaves the number unchanged.
- Dividing any number by 1 leaves the number unchanged.
- Multiplying any number by 0 results in the number 0.
- Adding 0 to any number leaves the number unchanged.
- Subtracting 0 from any number leaves the number unchanged.
- It's impossible, for purposes of SAT Math, to divide any number by 0.

Word problems

- SAT word problems are typically simple descriptions of one of the following:
    - Real-life situations
    - Abstract concepts
    - Example: An SAT word problem about a real-life situation might look like this:

> Joe buys two balloons for three dollars each, and a certain amount of candy. Each piece of the candy costs twenty-five cents. Joe gives the cashier ten dollars and receives twenty-five cents in change. How many pieces of candy did he buy?

- Example: An SAT word problem about an abstract concept might look like this:

> If *x* is the arithmetic mean of seven consecutive numbers, what is the median of those seven numbers?

- To solve SAT word problems, we have to transform them into math problems. These are the steps we follow to make that transformation:
  1. Note all the numbers given in the problem, and write them down on scratch paper.
  2. Identify key phrases and translate them into mathematical symbols for operations and variables. Use these to connect the numbers you wrote down in Step 1.
     - Example: In the phrase "two balloons for three dollars each," the *each* part means we have to *multiply* the two balloons by the three dollars in order to find out how much total money was spent on the two balloons. $2 * 3 = 6$. Six dollars were spent on the two balloons if they cost three dollars each.

- After the word problem has been translated into numbers and symbols, solve it like any other SAT Math problem (see the SAT Math Problem Completion Process).

Number lines
- A number line is a simple diagram that arranges numbers from least to greatest.
- The positions on a number line can be labeled with actual numbers or with variables.

  - Example: This number line shows all the integers from -7 to 4:

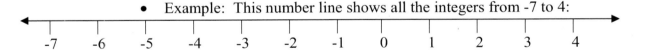

- On the SAT, number lines are drawn to scale and the tick marks are spaced evenly.
- The length of a number line between two numbers is the same thing as the distance between those two numbers.
- To determine the distance between two numbers on a number line, just subtract the number to the left from the number to the right.
  - Example: On the number line above, the distance between 1 and 3 is two units, which is the same thing as saying that $3 - 1 = 2$.

- On a number line, there is a DIFFERENCE between the distance that separates two numbers and the number of positions between them.
- If you're asked how many positions are BETWEEN two numbers on a number line, remember that you CANNOT answer this question by simply subtracting one number from the other—that's how you would find the distance. You should actually count the positions—you'll find the number of positions is one less than the difference you get when you subtract.

- Example: On the number line above, there are NOT two positions between the numbers 2 and 4, even though $4 - 2 = 2$. There is only one position between the numbers 2 and 4, which is one less than the difference we get when we subtract the number 2 from the number 4.

- On the SAT, the positions on a number line don't have to represent whole numbers. They might represent groups of five numbers at a time, or hundredths, or any other consistent amount.
- A number's absolute value is the distance of that number from zero on the number line.
    - Example: -4 and 4 both have an absolute value of 4. We signify the absolute value of a number with vertical lines on either side of the number: $|-4| = |4| = 4$.

Squares and square roots

- To square a number, multiply the number by itself.
  - Example: Five squared is five times five, or 5 * 5, or 25.

- To find the square root of a number, find the amount that has to be multiplied by itself in order to generate the number.
  - Example: The square root of 25 is the amount that yields 25 when it's multiplied by itself. As we just saw, that amount is 5. So the square root of 25 is 5.

- When you square any number, the result is always positive. This is because a positive number times a positive number gives a positive result, and so does a negative number times a negative number.
- Square roots on the SAT are always positive.
- The SAT never asks about the square root of a negative number.
- The SAT likes to ask about the squares of the numbers -12 through 12. Here they are:

Number	Square
-12 or 12	144
-11 or 11	121
-10 or 10	100
-9 or 9	81
-8 or 8	64
-7 or 7	49
-6 or 6	36
-5 or 5	25
-4 or 4	16
-3 or 3	9
-2 or 2	4
-1 or 1	1
0	0

- While we don't recommend using a calculator on the SAT if you can help it, remember that you can always find the square root of a number very easily on a good calculator.

Fractions and rational numbers

- A fraction is a special type of number that represents parts of a whole.
- Fractions are written this way:
  [number of parts being described in the situation]
  [number of parts that the whole is divided into]
  - Example: Imagine that we're sharing a six-pack of soda cans. I really like soda, so I drink five of the cans. In this situation, I've had five of the six cans that make up the six-pack—I've had 5/6 of the six-pack.

www.grammatix.com

- The number above the fraction bar is called a *numerator*.
- The number under the fraction bar is called a *denominator*.
- When the numerator of a fraction is less than the denominator, the value of the fraction is less than 1.
- When the numerator of a fraction is greater than the denominator, the value of the fraction is greater than 1.
  - Example: 1/2 is equal to one half, which is less than 1. 6/3 is equal to 2, which is greater than 1.

- Any integer can be thought of as having the denominator 1 already underneath it.
  - Example: 7 is the same thing as 7/1.

- A reciprocal is what you get if you switch the numerator and the denominator of a fraction.
  - Example: The reciprocal of 2/3 is 3/2. The reciprocal of 7 is 1/7. (Remember that all integers can be thought of as having the denominator 1.)

- To multiply two fractions, first multiply their numerators and write the new amount as the numerator of the new fraction; then, multiply the denominators and write the new amount as the denominator of the new fraction.
  - Example: 4/7 x 9/13 = 36/91

- To divide fraction *a* by fraction *b*, we actually multiply fraction *a* by the RECIPROCAL of fraction *b*.
  - Example: 4/7 divided by 9/13 = 4/7 x 13/9 = 52/63

- Multiplying a non-zero integer by a fraction that's less than 1 (that is, by a fraction where the numerator is less than the denominator) will give a result that is closer to zero on a number line than the original integer was. (Read this item again if you need to!)
  - Examples: 6 x 3/5 = 18/5, and 18/5 falls between 0 and 6 on a number line. -7 x 2/9 = -14/9, and -14/9 falls between -7 and 0 on a number line.

- Fraction *a* is equal to fraction *b* if you could multiply the numerator in *a* by a certain number to get the numerator in *b*, and you could also multiply the denominator in *a* by the same number to get the denominator of *b*.
  - Example: 3/5 is equal to 18/30 because 3 x 6 = 18 and 5 x 6 = 30. Here's another way to write this: 3/5 x 6/6 = 18/30. Notice that 6/6 is the same thing as 1 (six parts of a whole that's divided into six parts is the same thing as the whole itself). So all we really did here was multiply 3/5 by 1, and we know that doing this will give us an amount equal to 3/5.

- For more on fractions, see the discussion of factors and multiples below.

www.grammatix.com

Factors

- The factors of a number *x* are the positive integers that can be multiplied by each other to achieve that number *x*.
  - Example: The number 10 has the factors 5 and 2, because 5 * 2 = 10. It also has the factors 10 and 1, because 1 * 10 = 10.

- "Common factors," as the name suggests, are factors that two numbers have in common.
  - Example: The number 10 has the factors 1, 2, 5, and 10, as we just saw. The number 28 has the factors 1, 2, 4, 7, and 28. So the common factors of 10 and 28 are 1 and 2, because both 1 and 2 can be multiplied by positive integers to get both 10 and 28.

Multiples

- The multiples of a number *x* are the numbers you get when you multiply *x* by 1, 2, 3, 4, 5, and so on.
  - Example: The multiples of 4 are 4, 8, 12, 16, 20, 24, 28, 32, 36, 40, 44, 48, 52, and so on.

Remainders

- Remainders are what you get when you divide one number by another number and have something left over (this assumes you don't use fractions or decimals to write the answer to your division problem).
  - Example: If we divide 30 by 4, we see that it doesn't work out evenly. 4 * 7 = 28, which isn't enough, and 4 * 8 = 32, which is too much. So if we divide 30 by 4, one way to state the answer is to say that 30 divided by 4 is "7 with a remainder of 2," because 4 * 7 = 28 and 28 + 2 = 30.

- The remainder in a division problem must be less than the number we're dividing by.
  - Example: It doesn't make any sense to say that 30 divided by 4 is "3 with a remainder of 18," because 18 is bigger than 4 and 4 will still go into it a few more times.

- As a reminder, when you first learned to divide, you were probably taught to use remainders
- Most calculators don't give remainders when solving division problems—instead, they give fractions or decimals..

Prime numbers

- A prime number is a number that has exactly two factors: 1 and itself.
  - Example: 17 is a prime number because there are no positive integers besides 1 and 17 that can be multiplied by other integers to generate 17. (Try to come up with some—you won't be able to.)

- 24 is NOT a prime number because there are a lot of positive integers besides 1 and 24 that can be multiplied by other integers to generate 24. For example, 2, 4, 6, and 12 can all be multiplied by other integers to generate 24.
- All prime numbers are positive.
- The only even prime number is 2.
- 1 is NOT a prime number because it has only one factor (itself), while prime numbers must have exactly two factors.

Ratios, proportions, and percentages

- Ratios, proportions, and percentages are all ways to express a relationship between two numbers.
- A ratio is written as a pair of numbers with a colon between them.
  - Example: If you make 5 dollars for every 1 dollar I make, then the ratio of *your pay* to *my pay* is *5 : 1.*

- A proportion is usually written as a fraction, with a number in the numerator compared to the number in the denominator.
  - Examples: If you make 5 dollars for every 1 dollar I make, then your pay can be compared to my pay with the proportion 5/1. (Or, if we wanted to compare what I make to what you make, that proportion would be 1/5.)

- A percentage is a special proportion where one number is compared to 100.
- To determine a percentage, first compare two numbers with a proportion, and then divide the top number by the bottom number and multiply the result by 100.
  - Example: If I make 1 dollar for every 5 dollars you make, then the proportion that compares my pay to your pay is 1/5. If we divide 1 by 5 and multiply by 100, we see that I make 20% of what you make.

- Ratios can be set equal to each other and "cross-multiplied." (If you don't already know how to do this, don't worry—it's just a short cut around regular algebraic techniques.)
- If the relationship between two quantities is the kind where increasing one quantity results in an increase in the other quantity, then we say those two quantities "vary directly" or are "directly proportional."
  - Example: If I make 1 dollar for every 5 dollars you make, then when I make 4 dollars you make 20 dollars—increasing my pay to 4 leads to an increase in your pay to 20. That means our two rates of pay are in direct proportion.

- If two quantities are related so that increasing one decreases the other, then we say those two quantities "vary indirectly" or are "inversely proportional."
  - Example: If we have two quantities x and y set up so that $xy = 20$, then x and y are inversely proportional—every time one increases, the other one decreases, and vice-versa. So if x starts out as 10 and y starts out as 2, changing x to 5 means we have to change y to 4—as one decreases, the other increases.

Sequences

- Sequences are strings of numbers.
- On the SAT, the numbers in a sequence follow a rule or pattern.
- SAT sequences can either go on forever or stop at some point, depending on the setup of the question.
- There are two common types of SAT sequences, and we can classify them by the rules that are used to figure out which numbers go in the sequence. Let's look at the different types of SAT sequences:
  - Examples: The sequence 3, 5, 7, 9, 11, 13, . . . follows a very simple rule: to get the next number in the sequence, just add 2 to the number before. So the next number in this sequence would be 15, then 17, and so on.

    The sequence 3, 15, 75, 375, . . . also follows a simple rule: to get the next number, multiply the previous number by 5. The next number here would be 1,875.

- The SAT will NOT ask you to figure out the rule that a sequence follows.
- The Math section MIGHT ask you to figure out:
  - The sum of certain terms in a sequence
  - The average of certain terms.
  - The value of a specific term.

 If you studied sequences in school, they were probably a lot harder in your math class than they will be on the SAT. For example, there's no sigma notation on the SAT. (If you've never heard of sigma notation, don't worry about it.)

Set theory

- Sets are collections of things.
- Sets on the SAT are usually groups of numbers.
  - Example: The set of factors of 24 is [1, 2, 4, 6, 12, 24].

- On the SAT, the things in a set can be called "members" of that set or "elements" of that set.
- The "union" of two or more sets is what we get when we combine all of the members of those sets into a bigger set.
  - Example: The set of factors of 24 is [1, 2, 4, 6, 12, 24] and the set of factors of 36 is [1, 2, 3, 4, 6, 9, 12, 18, 36]. That means the union of those two sets is the set [1, 2, 3, 4, 6, 9, 12, 18, 24, 36].

- The "intersection" of two or more sets is the set of members that the two sets have in common.

- Example: Given the sets [1, 2, 4, 6, 12, 24] and [1, 2, 3, 4, 6 ,9, 12, 18, 36], the "intersection" is [1, 2, 4, 6, 12], because those members are common to both sets.

Counting problems

- On the SAT, "counting problems" are problems where you're asked to give the total number of ways that two or more events might happen.
- If you've studied these types of problems in math class, you probably called them "permutation and combination" problems.
- The general, basic rule of these types of problems is this: when you have two events, and the first event might happen in any one of x ways, and the second event might happen in any one of y ways, then the total number of ways that both events could happen together is given by xy. (That might sound a little complicated—let's do an example.)
  - Example: Imagine there are three roads between your house and your friend's house, and there are 6 roads between your friend's house and the library. If you're driving from your house to your friend's house and then to the library, how many different ways can you go?

    There are 3 ways to get from your house to your friend's house. So the event of you getting to your friend's house can happen in any one of 3 ways. Then there are 6 ways to get from your friend's house to the library, so the event of going to the library from the friend's house can happen in any one of 6 ways. The means the total number of paths you could travel from your house to your friend's house and then on to the library is given by 3 * 6, which is 18.

- The key to solving these types of problems is making sure you correctly count the number of possible outcomes for each event.
  - Example: Imagine that there are 3 roads between your house and your friend's house. You're going to visit her and then return home. For some reason, you can't travel the same road twice.

    What's the total number of ways you could go from your house to your friend's house and back? Well, the total number of ways to go from your house to your friend's house is 3, and the total number of ways to come back home is ONLY 2. Why can you only come back from your friend's house in 2 ways? *Because the rule of the problem says you're not allowed to use the same road twice, and when you go back home you will already have used one of the three roads to visit your friend in the first place.* So the right way to answer this is to multiply 3 by 2, NOT by 3. That means the answer is 6, NOT 9.

Operations on algebraic expressions

- Algebraic expressions are figures that include variables.
- Algebraic expressions, just like the regular numbers they represent, can be added, subtracted, multiplied, and divided—but sometimes there are special rules that apply.

- We can add or subtract two algebraic expressions when they involve the same variable expressions.
  - Example: We can add $5x$ and $19x$ to get $24x$, because the $5x$ and $19x$ both involve the same variable expression: x. We can subtract $17xyz^2$ from $100\, xyz^2$ and get $83xyz^2$ because they both involve the variable expression xyz^2.

    But if we want to add $5x$ to $17\, xyz^2$, we can't combine those two expressions any further because they have different variable expressions. So we would just write "$5x + 17xyz^2$" and leave it at that.

- We can multiply any two algebraic expressions by multiplying all the terms in the first expression by all the terms in the second expression.
  - Example: $5x * 7y = 35xy$

    $(5a + 2)(4b + 9) = 20ab + 45a + 8b + 18$

- We can divide any algebraic expression by another algebraic expression when they share factors. (See the discussion on factoring algebraic expressions.)
  - Example: $26xy/13x = 2y$

- When multiplying two algebraic expressions on the SAT, we can often use the "FOIL" technique. "FOIL" stands for "First, Outer, Inner, Last," and refers to the order in which the terms of the two expressions are multiplied by one another.
- You have probably used FOIL in your math classes, but if you used some other technique there's no need to worry.
  - Example: To multiply the expressions $(5x + 7)$ and $(3x + 4)$, we can use FOIL.

    The "First" pair in the acronym is the $5x$ and the $3x$, because they are the first terms in each expression. We multiply these and get $15x^2$.

    The "Outer" pair in the acronym is the $5x$ and the 4. We multiply these and get $20x$.

    The "Inner" pair in the acronym is the 7 and the $3x$. We multiply these and get $21x$.

    The "Last" pair in the acronym is the 7 and the 4. We multiply these and get 28.

    Now we just add up all those terms and we get the expression $15x^2 + 20x + 21x + 28$, which we can simplify a little bit by combining the two like x terms, giving us:

    $15x^2 + 41x + 28.$

    So $(5x + 7)(3x + 4) = 15x^2 + 41x + 28$

IMPORTANT! If this seems a little complicated now, don't worry about it. You'll get i
practice—and there isn't that much of it on the SAT anyway.

Factoring algebraic expressions

- On the SAT, factoring an algebraic expression involves breaking the expression
  into two other expressions that could be multiplied by each other to give the origi
  expression.
    - Example: If we have an algebraic expression like $(8x + 4)$, we can break th
      down into the factors 4 and $(2x + 1)$, because $4(2x + 1) = 8x + 4$.

- On the SAT, there are three types of factoring situations you'll need to recognize:
    - Recognizing common factors involves noticing that every term in a given
      expression has a common factor, as we did in the last example.
    - Example: In the expression $(21xy + 7x)$, both of the terms in the expression
      have a common factor of $7x$, so we can factor the expression like this: $7x(3y + 1)$.

    - Factoring polynomials basically involves doing the "FOIL" process in reverse.
      Trust me, it's not as hard as it looks. It just takes a little practice.
    - Example: $9x^2 - 21x + 12 = (3x - 3)(3x - 4)$

      $5x^2 - 3x - 2 = (5x + 2)(x - 1)$

    - When we factor the difference of two squares, there's a shortcut we can us —
      the difference of two squares can be factored as the product of the sum of the
      square roots of the two squares times the difference of the square roots of the
      two squares. Let's see an example.
    - Example: $9x^2 - 4 = (3x + 2)(3x - 2)$

Exponents

- An exponent of a number is what we get when we multiply the number by itself a
  certain number of times.
    - Example: $x * x * x = x^3$ is an example of an exponential expression. The 3 in
      this example is the exponent, and the x is called the "base."

- Exponents can be positive or negative.
- When an exponent is positive, we multiply the base by itself as many times as the
  exponent indicates, just like we did in the above example.
- When an exponent is negative, we treat it just like a positive exponent EXCEPT that
  we take the reciprocal of the final amount (take another look at the discussion of
  reciprocals on page).

www.grammatix.com

- Example: $x^5 = x * x * x * x * x$

$x^{-5} = 1/(x^5)$

We can multiply exponent expressions by each other when the bases are identical. To do that, we just add the exponents:
- Example: $(x^7)(x^4) = (x * x * x * x * x * x * x) (x * x * x * x) =$
$x * x * x * x * x * x * x * x * x * x * x = x^{11}$

$(x^7)(x^{-4}) = x^3$

We can also divide exponent expressions when they have the same base. For that we just subtract the exponents:
- Example: $(x^8)/(x^2) = x^6$

Finally, we can raise exponential expressions to other exponents by multiplying the first exponent by the second one:
- Example: $(x^4)^5 = x^{20}$

Note that raising any number to an exponent of zero gives you the number 1.
- Example: $y^0 = 1$

Using equations

On the SAT, an equation is a statement that involves an algebraic expression and an equals sign.
- Example: $5x = 20$ is an equation, because it involves the algebraic expression $5x$ and an equals sign.

Solving an equation means figuring out how much the variable in the equation is worth. We can solve equations just like you learned in algebra class—by multiply, dividing, adding, or subtracting both sides of the equation by the same amounts until we're left with a value for the variable.
- Example: $5x = 20$
$5x/5 = 20/5$
$x = 4$

On the SAT, we can often use equations to answer a question *even when we can't solve the equation.*
- Example: We might be told that $(a + b)/10 = 15$. How can we figure out the value of $a + b$? Ordinarily, you might try to figure out a first, and then b, and then add them together. But we don't have enough information to do that. So what can we do? Well, we just solve for the entire amount $a + b$. In this situation, we can do that by multiplying both sides by 10, so $a + b = 150$.

www.grammatix.com

- On the SAT, we can also solve equations "in terms of" one particular variable. To do this, we just isolate the target variable on one side of the equation.
    - Example: What if we have to solve this expression in terms of n?

$$4n + 7y = 2a$$
$$4n = 2a - 7y$$
$$n = (2a - 7y)/4$$
$$n = (2a - 7y)/4$$

- Sometimes you'll have a "system" of equations. A system of equations contains two or more equations with the same variables.
    - Example: This is a system of equations:

$$x + y = 5$$
$$2x - y = 7$$

- The easiest way to solve a system of equations is to solve one equation in terms of one variable, like we just did before. Then we substitute in the second equation and solve.
    - Example: First, we'll isolate the y in the first equation, giving us that equation in terms of y: $y = 5 - x$. Now that we know y is the same thing as $5 - x$, we just plug in $5 - x$ where y appears in the second equation:

$$2x - (5 - x) = 7$$
$$2x - 5 + x = 7$$
$$3x - 5 = 7$$
$$3x = 12$$
$$x = 4$$

Now that we know x is 4, we just plug that back into the first equation, and we'll be able to solve for y:

$$(4) + y = 5$$
$$y = 1$$

Inequalities

- On the SAT, inequalities are statements that show a particular amount may be greater than or less than a second amount. They use these symbols:
    - The symbol $<$ means "less than."
    - The symbol $>$ means "greater than."
    - The symbol $\leq$ means "less than or equal to."
    - The symbol $\geq$ means "greater than or equal to."
- You solve an inequality the same way you solve an equation, with one difference: when you multiply by -1 to solve for a variable, you have to switch the direction of the inequality symbol.
    - Example:

$$-x/4 = 10 \qquad\qquad -x/4 \leq 10$$
$$-x = 10(4) \qquad\qquad -x \leq 10(4)$$
$$-x = 40 \qquad\qquad -x \leq 40$$
$$\qquad\qquad\qquad\qquad x \geq -40$$

www.grammatix.com

Solving quadratic equations by factoring

- A quadratic equation is an equation that involves three terms:
  - one term is a variable expression raised to the power of 2.
  - one term is a variable expression not raised to any power.
  - one term is a regular number with no variable.
  - Example: $x^2 + 3x = -2$ is a quadratic equation because it involves a term with x squared, a term with x, and a regular number.

- There is only one way to solve quadratic equations on the SAT, and that is by factoring. (See the discussion of factoring above).
- To solve a quadratic equation by factoring, we have to make one side of the equation equal to zero, and then factor the other side of the equation (the quadratic part).
  - Example:
  $$x^2 + 3x \qquad = -2$$
  $$x^2 + 3x + 2 \quad = 0$$
  $$(x + 1)(x + 2) = 0$$

    Now that we know $(x + 1)(x + 2) = 0$, what else do we know? We know that one of those two factors has to equal zero—either $x + 1 = 0$ or $x + 2 = 0$. How do we know this? Remember that the only way to multiply two numbers and get zero is if one of the numbers is zero. So if we can multiply $x + 1$ by $x + 2$ and get zero, then either $x + 1$ is zero or $x + 2$ is zero.

    Once we've factored, we solve for the variable by creating two small sub-equations in which each factor is set equal to zero.
    $$x + 1 = 0 \quad \text{or} \quad x + 2 = 0$$
    $$x \qquad = -1 \quad \text{or} \quad x \qquad = -2$$

    So in the equation $x^2 + 3x = -2$, x can equal either -1 or -2.

IMPORTANT! Quadratic equations can have multiple solutions, as we've just seen.

Functions

- Functions are formulas that tell you how to generate one number by using another number.
- Functions can be written in a lot of ways. On the SAT, they'll usually be written in $f(x)$ notation, also called "function notation."
  - Example: $f(x) = x^3 + 4$ is a function written in function notation.

- When we write with function notation, we don't have to use $f(x)$ specifically. We could write $g(n)$, $a(b)$, or whatever.

www.grammatix.com

IMPORTANT! Don't confuse function notation like $f(x)$ with the multiplicative expression $(f)(x)$, which means "f times x"!

- When we evaluate a function for a certain number x, it means that we plug the number x into the function and see what the $f(x)$ is.
  - Example: If our function is $f(x) = x^3 + 4$ and we want to evaluate the function where $x = 2$, then we get this:
  $$f(x) = x^3 + 4$$
  $$f(2) = (2)^3 + 4$$
  $$f(2) = 8 + 4$$
  $$f(2) = 12$$

- So for our function, when x equals 2, the $f(x)$ equals 12.
- The "domain" of a function is the set of numbers on a number line where the function can be evaluated.
  - Example: In the function $f(x) = x^3 + 4$, the domain is all the numbers on the number line, because we can put any value from the number line in for x and get a result for $f(x)$.

  - In the function $f(x) = \sqrt{x}$, the domain is only those numbers that can have a square root. Remember that, on the SAT, you can't take the square root of a negative number. That means the domain for the function $f(x) = \sqrt{x}$ is the set of non-negative numbers.

- The "range" of a function is the set of numbers that $f(x)$ can come out equal to.
  - Example: The function $f(x) = x^3 + 4$ has a range of negative infinity to positive infinity—by putting in the right thing for x, we can get any number we want as $f(x)$.

  The function $f(x) = \sqrt{x}$ has a range of only non-negative numbers, because there is no way to put any number as x and get a number for $f(x)$ that's negative.

Linear functions
- A point can be plotted on a graph in (x, y) notation if we take the x number and make it the horizontal separation between the point (x, y) and the origin $(0, 0)$, and then we make the y value the vertical separation between (x, y) and $(0, 0)$.
- A linear function is a function in which the $f(x)$ is replaced with a y, and each (x, y) pairing given by the function is plotted on a graph.
- All the (x, y) pairings in a linear function form a straight line when they're plotted on the graph.
  - Example: The function $f(x) = (x/2) + 1$ is linear, because all of the (x, y) pairings that it generates fall in a straight line when they're plotted as lines on a

graph.

Here's a chart that shows some (x, y) pairings for the function $f(x) = (x/2) + 1$:

x	y
0	1
1	1.5
2	2
3	2.5
4	3
5	3.5
6	4
7	4.5
8	5
9	5.5
10	6
11	6.5
12	7
13	7.5
14	8
15	8.5
16	9

When we plot these points on a graph, we see that they fall in a straight line:

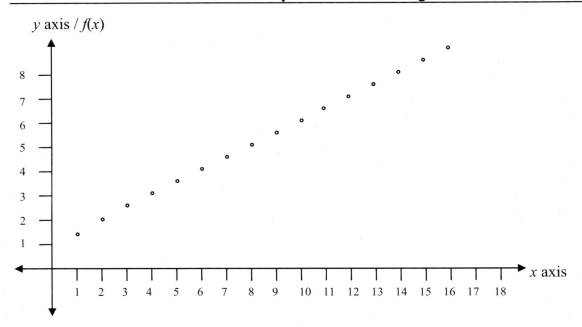

Of course, the points plotted on the graph are only the (x, y) pairings when x is a positive integer. But isn't the domain for $f(x) = (x/2) + 1$ all the numbers on the number line? That means that there must be an $f(x)$ even where x equals 1.135623 or 8.4453. For every point on the x axis, there's a corresponding $f(x)$ on the y axis. We could "connect the dots" on our graph above, and extend the line of our function infinitely in either direction. Let's do that:

www.grammatix.com

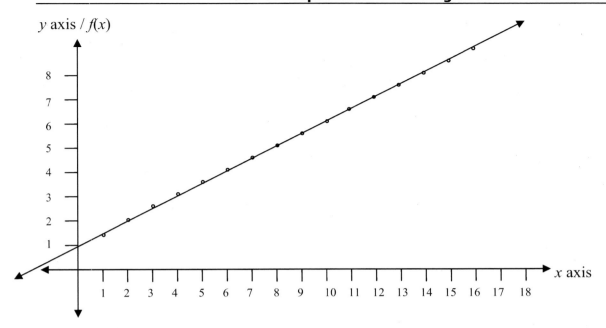

- The "slope" of a linear function is a fraction that shows you how steeply the line is tilted. To find the slope of a line, choose any two points on the line. Measure the vertical separation between the two points, *starting from the left-most point*. The vertical separation number goes in the numerator of the slope fraction. Then measure the horizontal separation between the two points, again starting from the left-most point. The horizontal separation goes in the denominator of the slope fraction.
  - Example: In our graph above, we might pick any two points on the function line to determine the slope—let's pick (2,2) and (8,5). The vertical separation here is the difference between 2 on the left-most point and 5 on the right-most point. So the vertical separation here is 3, and we put a 3 in the numerator of the slope fraction for this line. Now we determine the horizontal separation between 2 on the left and 8 on the right, which is 6. So a 6 goes in the denominator of the slope fraction. Now we have the numerator and the denominator of the slope fraction, and we see that the entire slope fraction is 3/6, or 1/2. So the slope of $f(x) = (x/2) + 1$ is 1/2. (Keep reading for a much easier way to figure out slope.)

- The function for a line will often be written in this format: $y = mx + b$. In fact, our function from the previous example was written in that way: $f(x) = (x/2) + 1$. (Remember that y and $f(x)$ are the same thing for the purposes of graphing a function, and that "½ x" can be re-written as $x/2$.)
- This $y = mx + b$ format is called "slope-intercept format." We call it that because it shows us two things right away: the slope of the function, and the "y-intercept" of the function.
  - The m coefficient of the x variable will be the slope.
  - The b constant in the function will be the point where the linear function crosses the y axis.

- Example: In the linear function $f(x) = 9/7\,x + 14$, the m in the $y = mx + b$ notation is 9/7, and the b is 14. This means the slope of the function is 9/7, and the point where the line crosses the y-axis is 14.

  In the linear function $y = -3/2\,x + 2$, the slope is -3/2 and the y-intercept is 2.

- When two linear functions have the same slope, they are parallel.
- When you can multiply the slope of one linear function by the slope of another linear function and get -1, the two linear functions are perpendicular to one another.
- The SAT will never ask you to graph a linear function. It will only ask you to use graphs to figure out other information, or to identify an answer choice that correctly graphs a function.

Quadratic functions
- A quadratic function is a function where the x variable has an exponent of 2.
  - Example: $y = x^2$

- Quadratic functions are NEVER linear.
- The SAT never asks you to draw the graph of a quadratic function. It will only ask you to use given graphs to answer questions, or to identify which answer choice correctly graphs a given function.
- Quadratic functions always extend infinitely in some direction (up or down).
  - Example: The graph of $y = x^2$ extends "up" infinitely, and looks like this:

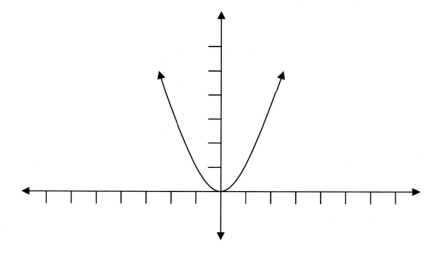

The graph of $y = -(x^2)$ extends "down" infinitely, and looks like this:

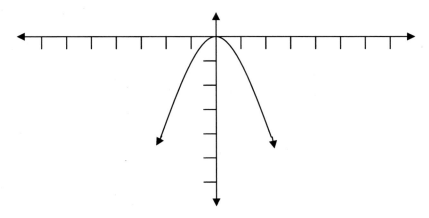

 Note that the "direction" of the graph of a quadratic equation is really just a question of its range. When the range extends to negative infinity, the graph points "down." When the range extends to positive infinity, the graph points "up."

- When a quadratic function points down, its highest point is the (x, y) pair that has the greatest y value,
- When a quadratic function points up, its lowest point is the (x, y) pair that has the lowest y value.
- Sometimes you'll be asked to find the "zeros" of a quadratic function. The zeros are the points where the graph of the function intercepts the x-axis. To find the zeros, just set $f(x)$ equal to zero, and then solve the resulting equation by factoring, just like we did above.
  - Example: To find the zeros of $f(x) = (x^2)/3 - 3$, we set $f(x)$ equal to zero and then solve for x by factoring:
    $0 = (x^2)/3 - 3$
    $3 = (x^2)/3$
    $9 = x^2$
    $x = 3 \ \ or \ \ x = -3$
    So the zeros of $f(x) = (x^2)/3 - 3$ are 3 and -3.

Geometric notation
- The SAT likes to use what it calls "geometric notation" to describe lines, rays, angles, and so on. You've probably seen this notation in your classes, but don't worry if you haven't—it's not hard to learn.

Examples:
AB means the distance from A to B.

www.grammatix.com

$\overleftrightarrow{AB}$ means the line that goes through points A and B (note the little arrows on the ends, which indicate an infinite extension into space.)

$\overline{AB}$ means the line segment with endpoints A and B. (The lack of arrowheads on the symbol indicates that the given segment does not stretch on to infinity.)

$\overrightarrow{AB}$ means the ray with endpoint A that goes through B and then stretches on infinitely.

$\overrightarrow{BA}$ means the ray with B for an endpoint that goes through A and stretches on infinitely.

$\angle ABC$ means the angle with point B as a vertex that has point A on one leg and point C on the other.

$m\angle ABC$ means the measure of the angle with point B as a vertex, and with point A on one leg and point C on the other.

$\triangle ABC$ means the triangle with vertices A, B, and C.

$\square ABCD$ means the quadrilateral with vertices A, B, C, and D.

$\overline{AB} \perp \overline{BC}$ means that the line segments AB and BC are perpendicular to each other.

Points and lines

- A unique line can be drawn to connect any two points.
- Between any two points on a line, there is a midpoint that is halfway between the two points.
- Any three or more points may or may not fall on the same line. If they do, we say the points are collinear.

Angles in the plane

- Degrees are the units that we use to measure how "wide" or "big" an angle is.
    - Examples:
        This is a 45-degree angle:

www.grammatix.com

- This is a 90-degree angle, also called a "right angle:"

- This is a 180-degree angle, which is the same thing as a straight line:

- Sometimes angles have special relationships. The two types of special relationships that the SAT cares about the most are vertical angles and supplementary angles
- Vertical angles are the pairs of angles that lie across from each other when two lines intersect. In a pair of vertical angles, the two angles have the same degree measurements as each other.
  - Example: Angles $\angle$ABC and $\angle$DBE are a pair of vertical angles, so they have the same degree measurement. Angles $\angle$ABD and $\angle$CBE are also a pair of vertical angles, so they have the same degree measurements as each other as well.

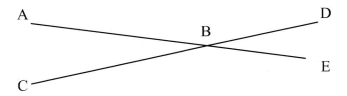

- Supplementary angles are pairs of angles whose measurements add up to 180 degrees. When supplementary angles are next to each other, they form a straight line.
  - Example: $\angle$ACD and $\angle$ACB are a pair of supplementary angles, because their measurements together add up to 180 degrees—together, they form the straight line BD.

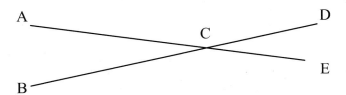

www.grammatix.com

Triangles

- The SAT loves to ask about triangles. The more you know about them, the better your score will be.
- The sum of the measures of the angles in any triangle is 180 degrees, the same as it is in a straight line.
- In any triangle, the longest side is always opposite the biggest angle, and the shortest side is always opposite the smallest angle.
- In an "equilateral" triangle, all the sides are the same length.
- In an equilateral triangle, all the angles measure 60 degrees each.
    - Example: In the equilateral triangle $\triangle$EQI below, all the sides are of equal length, and all the angles are 60 degrees.

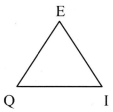

- In an "isosceles" triangle, two of the three sides are the same length as each other, and two of the three angles are the same size as each other.
    - Example: In the isosceles triangle $\triangle$ISO below, side $\overline{IS}$ is the same length as side $\overline{SO}$. Also, $S\!\!\!/O$ and $S\!\!\!/I$ have the same degree measurement as each other.

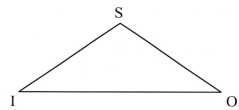

- A "right" triangle is a triangle that includes a ninety-degree angle as one of its three angles.
- A special relationship exists between the measurements of the sides of a right triangle: If you take the lengths of the two shorter sides and square them, and then add those two squares together, the resulting amount is the square of the length of the longest side.

    - Example: In the right triangle below, $a^2 + b^2 = c^2$

- The expression of this relationship, $a^2 + b^2 = c^2$, is called the "Pythagorean Theorem."

www.grammatix.com

- A "Pythagorean triple" is a set of three numbers that can all be the lengths of the sides of the same right triangle. Memorizing four of these sets will make your life easier on the SAT.
  - Example: $\{3, 4, 5\}$ is a Pythagorean triple because $3^2 + 4^2 = 5^2$.
    $\{1, 1, \sqrt{2})$ is a Pythagorean triple because $1^2 + 1^2 = \sqrt{2}^2$
    $\{1, \sqrt{3}, 2\}$ is a Pythagorean triple because $1^2 + \sqrt{3}^2 = 2^2$
    $\{5, 12, 13\}$ is a Pythagorean triple because $5^2 + 12^2 = 13^2$

- When we multiply each number in a Pythagorean triple by the same number, we get another Pythagorean triple.
  - Example: If we know $\{3, 4, 5\}$ is a Pythagorean triple, then we also know $\{6, 8, 10\}$ is a Pythagorean triple, because $\{6, 8, 10\}$ is what we get when we multiply every number in $\{3, 4, 5\}$ by 2.

- In a $\{1, 1, \sqrt{2}\}$ right triangle, the angle measurements are $45°, 45°, 90°$.
- In a $\{1, \sqrt{3}, 2\}$ right triangle, the angle measurements are $30°, 60°, 90°$.
- Two triangles are "similar triangles" if they have all the same angle measurements.
- Between two similar triangles, the relationship between any two corresponding sides is the same as between any other two corresponding sides.
  - Example: Triangles $\triangle ABC$ and $\triangle DEF$ below are similar. Side $\overline{AB}$ has length 8, and side $\overline{DE}$ has length 24, so every side measurement in $\triangle DEF$ must be three times the corresponding side in $\triangle AB$

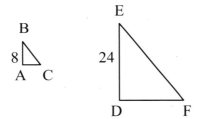

- The formula for the area of a triangle is given in the front of every real SAT Math section.
- In every triangle, the length of each side must be less than the sum of the lengths of the other sides. (Otherwise, the triangle would not be able to "close.")

Parallelograms
- A parallelogram is a four-sided figure where both pairs of opposite sides are parallel to each other.
- In a parallelogram, opposite angles are equal to each other, and the measures of all the angles added up together equal 360.

- Example: In ⬜ABCD below, all the interior angles taken together equal 360°, and opposite angles have equal measurements.

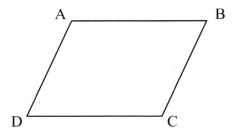

Rectangles

- Rectangles are special parallelograms where all the angles measure 90 degrees. In a rectangle, if you know the lengths of the sides then you can always figure out the length from one corner to the opposite corner by using the Pythagorean theorem.

- Example: In the rectangle below, all angles are right angles, and we can use the Pythagorean theorem to determine that the diagonal AC must have a length of 13, since $5^2 + 12^2 = 13^2$.

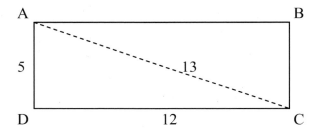

Squares

- Squares are special rectangles where all the sides have equal length.

Area

- The area of a two-dimensional figure is the amount of two-dimensional space that the figure covers.
- Area is always measured in square units.
- All the area formulas you need for the SAT appear in the beginning of each Math section, so there's no need to memorize them—you just need to know how to use them.

Perimeters (squares, rectangles, circles)

- The perimeter of a two-dimensional object is the sum of the lengths of its sides or, for a circle, the distance around the circle.
- The perimeter of a circle is called the "circumference."
- To find the perimeter of a non-circle, just add up the lengths of the sides.

- The formula for the circumference of a circle appears in the beginning of every real SAT Math section.

Other polygons

- The SAT might give you questions about special polygons, like pentagons, hexagons, octagons, and so on.
- The sum of the angle measurements of any polygon can be determined with a simple formula: Where s is the number of sides of the polygon, the sum of the angle measurements is $(s - 2) * 180$.
  - Examples: A triangle has 3 sides, so the sum of its angle measurements is given by $(3 - 2) * 180$, which is the same thing as $(1) * 180$, which is the same thing as 180. So the sum of the measurements of the angles in a triangle is 180 degrees. (Remember that we already knew this!)

- A hexagon has 6 sides, so the sum of its angle measurements is $(6 - 2) * 180$, or $(4) * 180$, which is 720. So all the angles in a hexagon add up to 720 degrees.
- To find the perimeter of any polygon, just add up the lengths of the sides.
- To find the area of a polygon besides a triangle or parallelogram, just divide the polygon into smaller triangles and find the areas of the triangles. A real SAT math question will always lend itself to this solution nicely.

Circles (diameter, radius, arc, tangents, circumference, area)

- A circle is the set of points in a particular plane that are all equidistant from a single point, called the center.
  - Example: Circle O has a center point O and consists of all the points in one plane that are 5 units away from the center:

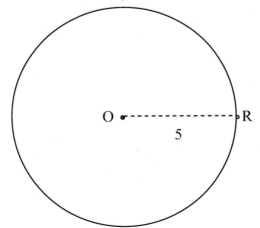

$$O \,\bullet\text{-}\text{-}\text{-}\text{-}\text{-}\text{-}\text{-}\text{-}\text{-}\text{-}\text{-}\text{-}\text{-}\!\!\blacktriangleright R$$
$$5$$

- A radius is a line segment drawn from the center point of a circle to the edge of the circle.
  - Example: In the circle above, the line segment OR is a radius because it stretches from the center of the circle (O) to the edge of the circle.

- All the radii of a circle have the same length, since all the points on the edge of the circle are the same distance from the center point.

www.grammatix.com

- A diameter is a line segment drawn from one edge of a circle, through the center of the circle, all the way to the opposite edge.
  - Example: LR is a diameter of circle *O* because it starts at one edge of the circle, stretches through the center of the circle, and stops at the opposite edge of the circle.

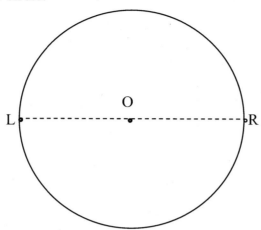

- Because a diameter can be broken into two opposite radii, a diameter always has a length equal to twice the radius of the circle.
- A diameter of a circle is the longest line segment that can be drawn through the circle.
- A tangent line is a line that intersects a circle at only one point.
- A tangent line is perpendicular to the radius of the circle that ends at the one point shared by the tangent and the circle.
  - Example: Circle *O* has a tangent line TS that intersects the circle at point R, and is perpendicular to radius OR.

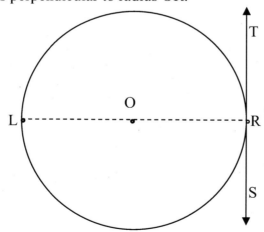

- The circumference of a circle is the length around the circle, similar to the perimeter of a polygon.

- An arc is a portion of a circle. We can measure an arc by drawing radii to the endpoints of the arc, and then measuring the angle formed by the radii at the center of the circle.
  - Example: Circle O has a 90° arc PR, which we can measure by measuring the angle formed by radius PO and radius RO.

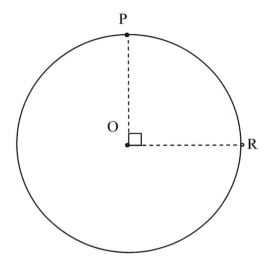

- The formulas for area and circumference of a circle appear in the beginning of all real SAT math sections, so there's no need to memorize them.

Solid geometry
- On the SAT, solid geometry may involve cubes, rectangular solids, prisms, cylinders, cones, spheres, or pyramids.
- All necessary volume formulas will be given to you, so there's no need to memorize them.
- The surface area of a solid is the sum of the areas of its faces (except for spheres or other "rounded" solids, which you won't have to worry about on the SAT).

Statistics
- The arithmetic mean of a set of numbers is the result you get when you add all the numbers together and then divide by the number of things that you added.
  - Example: The average of $\{4, 9, 92\}$ is 35, because $(4 + 9 + 92)/3 = 35$.

- The median of a set of numbers is the number that appears in the middle of the set when all the numbers in the set are arranged from least to greatest.
  - Example: The median of $\{4, 9, 92\}$ is 9, because when we arrange the three numbers from least to greatest, 9 is in the middle.

- If there is an even number of elements in the set, then the median of that set is the arithmetic mean of the two numbers in the middle of the set when the elements of the set are arranged from least to greatest.
- The mode of a set of numbers is the number that appears most frequently in the set.

- Example: The mode of {7, 7, 23, 44} is 7, because 7 appears more often than any other number in the set.

Probability (elementary and geometric)

- The probability of an event is a fraction that describes how likely the event is to happen. If the fraction is closer to 1, the event is more likely to happen; if the fraction is closer to zero, the event is less likely to happen.
- To determine the fraction, you first calculate the total number of possible outcomes and place this number in the denominator of the fraction; then, you determine the number of outcomes that satisfy the event's requirements, and place this number in the numerator of the fraction.
    - Example: The probability of rolling a 3 on a normal 6-sided die is 1/6. There are 6 possible outcomes, so 6 goes in the denominator of the fraction. Out of those 6 outcomes we only want one, the one where a 3 comes up, so 1 goes in the numerator of the fraction.

- The probability of rolling an odd number on a normal 6-sided die is 3/6. Again, there are 6 possible numbers we might roll, so 6 is our denominator. But now, since we want any odd number, the numbers 1, 3, and 5 all satisfy the requirements of our event, so there are 3 possible outcomes that we'll be happy with—that means 3 goes in the numerator.
- Probability fractions can be manipulated just like any other fractions.
- To find the probability of two or more events happening in a sequence, we just find the probabilities of each event by itself, and then multiply them by each other.
    - Example: The probability of rolling double-sixes on two normal 6-sided dice is 1/36, because the probability of rolling a six on either die is 1/6, and (1/6)(1/6) = 1/36.

The Rules for SAT Math

The rules for SAT Math Problems are pretty much the same, whether you're looking at Multiple Choice Questions or Student-Produced Response Questions. You must know the rules if you want to succeed!

SAT Math Rule 1: You Have to Know the Words

In the Verbal section, you can usually fake your way past a few unfamiliar words in a particular question by using context and hidden patterns—the Strategy Guides for those question types explain how to do this. But if an SAT Math question asks you about the number of prime factors in a set, there's no way to answer the question without knowing what prime factors are. The questions don't really have any context. You have to know the terminology.

SAT Math Rule 2: You Don't Have to Know Formulas

You DON'T have to know any formulas, but you DO have to know when to USE particular formulas. For example, the SAT may want you to realize that you need to find the area of a triangle, but it won't ask you to know the formula. The test provides EVERY SINGLE FORMULA that you need to answer every question.

SAT Math Rule 3: All SAT Math is Easy

All the math on the SAT Math section is relatively easy.

In advanced high school math problems, the solution to one problem might involve complex graphs, trigonometric expressions, fraction bars, and pi; they're very complex problems, and they have very complex answers.

On the SAT, the solution is much more likely to be a plain old number like 12. The math is relatively simple, so the solution is relatively simple.

SAT Math Rule 4: The Drawings are Usually Accurate

You can assume that every drawing is done to scale EXCEPT when the test specifically says otherwise. This is a very useful fact, because it sometimes lets you answer questions just by measuring things—you don't need any math at all.

SAT Math Rule 5: Limited Subject-Matter

In a few moments, we'll go over every single mathematical concept the SAT might throw at you. You'll find that you're familiar with most of them, if not all of them, and the rest are relatively straightforward. Once you know these concepts, you can rest assured that they will be enough to answer *every single real SAT question*.

SAT Math Rule 6: 30 Seconds or Less

The most important rule of all, from a strategic perspective, is that EVERY SINGLE MATH QUESTION can be answered in less than 30 seconds!

This doesn't mean that you're stupid if it takes you longer—it just means you aren't going about answering a question in the easiest way. When you're looking for a way to solve the problem, just remember that every single question is simple, no matter how complicated it may seem at first.

SAT Math Rule 7: All Necessary Information

One of the most important things to remember is that each question has all the information you need in order to solve it—no matter how much it might seem like that isn't true.

The Hidden Patterns of SAT Math Questions

Most of the hidden patterns on the SAT Math section have to do with using the answer choices to help you check your answers, where that's possible. Looking at the answer choices can reassure you that you have the right answer (or show you your mistakes so you can correct them).

Hidden Pattern 1: Halves and Doubles

Very often, one of the wrong answer choices will be twice as much as the right answer choice, or half as much as it. This is especially true when the problem involves multiplying or dividing an amount by 2. If you solve a problem and get an answer like 18, a wrong answer choice like 36 might reassure you that you're right.

Remember that this pattern is an indication that you're probably right, not a confirmation that you're definitely right. Also, it's important not to get it backwards—in the same hypothetical example, the right answer might be 36, and the wrong answer might be 18! Be very aware of this useful pattern, but don't rely on it exclusively.

Hidden Pattern 2: Right Answer, Wrong Time

One of the ways that the SAT will try to confuse you is by giving you a problem that involves two or three steps. When it does that, one of the wrong answers will usually be the number that you would get if you stopped after one of the earlier steps. For example, a problem might ask you to find the price for pens by giving you the prices for different combinations of pens, pencils, and erasers. The problem might require you to figure out the price of pencils in order to figure out the price for pens, and one of the wrong answer choices would be the price for pencils. Because this wrong answer is actually a number that you found in the process of solving the problem, it can reassure you that you're on the right track.

Hidden Pattern 3: Substitution

Like we said before, the SAT likes to give you problems that look complicated but have very simple solutions. The test is most likely to do this by showing you a rather complicated expression that you can simplify by substituting one thing for another. If you start looking for substitution opportunities, you'll find them all over the test, and they'll make your life easier.

www.grammatix.com
Page 95

SAT Math Problem Completion Process

Now that we've explained the rules and patterns that you'll find on the SAT Math section, we can look at the process that I recommend for those questions.

1. Identify the words in the Math Question that you don't know.

[If you know all the words, proceed to Step 2.]

[If you don't know all the words, there's almost no chance that you'll answer the question correctly. Skip it and move on to the next question.]

2. Draw a diagram.

In your test booklet, draw a diagram of the situation described in the question. This "diagram" could be a sketch of a rectangle, an equation described in the question, a simple drawing, or anything else. DRAW A DIAGRAM EVEN IF ONE IS ALREADY PROVIDED BY THE TEST. There are two reasons for this:

- Reproducing the diagram will force you to notice everything in the question. You can't redraw something without noticing it!
- The SAT often provides incomplete diagrams that don't show everything described in the question. If you redraw the diagram and add all the information in the text, the solution often becomes obvious.

There's one important thing that you absolutely can't forget in the process of drawing your diagram—you absolutely must NOT make any mistakes! If you draw a bad diagram, you'll end up choosing the wrong answer choice, which defeats the purpose of drawing the diagram at all. As long as you pay attention to the question when you make your diagram, you'll find it a very useful tool.

3. Use the diagram.

Now that you have your diagram (or equation or sketch or whatever), try to figure out what's going on with the question. In other words, determine two things:

- what the question is describing
- what it wants you to figure out

The better your "diagram," the easier this will be!

4. Using the toolbox, figure out a 30-second solution.

Remember the "toolbox" we went over before? It contained every single mathematical concept you might need for the SAT. Your job in this step is to use the relevant concepts from the toolbox in order to connect the prompt to the correct answer. And don't forget—the best solutions will take you less than 30 seconds to work out.

This step will force you to find a simple, fast solution to the problem. In order to do this, you'll need to use your diagram and have a good understanding of what the question is all about. In general, the fastest solutions require very little "math." Fast solutions usually involve knowing the properties of various mathematical terms.

- Fast solutions to Multiple-Choice Problems will often involve using the answer choices to help you get to the answer.

- Fast solutions to Student-Produced Response Problems will often involve identifying one specific correct answer out of a set of correct answers.

```
[If you can figure out a way to solve the problem in less than 30
seconds, go to Step 5.]
```

```
[If you can't figure out a way to solve the problem in less than 30
seconds, skip the problem and come back to it when you've answered
all the other questions.]
```

5. Solve the problem.

After you have read the question, diagrammed it, fully understood it, and figured out a way to solve it quickly, you can go ahead and carry out your solution. IF YOU TRY TO SOLVE THE PROBLEM WITHOUT GOING THROUGH THE EARLIER STEPS, YOU'LL JUST WASTE YOUR TIME.

6. Go through the answer choices.

Figure out why the SAT has included each answer choice. In other words, see if you can figure out the mistake you would have to make in order to come up with each wrong answer choice. Be on the lookout for hidden patterns like the ones we talked about.

If you're fully satisfied that you know why your answer is right and why the other answers are wrong (for multiple choice questions), mark your answer and move on to the next question. AS ALWAYS, IF YOU'RE NOT COMPLETELY SURE THAT YOU HAVE THE RIGHT ANSWER, SKIP THE QUESTION. DON'T GUESS! If you don't remember why you shouldn't guess, go back and look at our discussion of the problems with guessing.

SAT Math Problem Completion Process Conclusion

That's all there is to SAT Math questions!

The important thing about SAT Math questions is that you shouldn't try to solve them without setting them up first. Taking a few seconds to put together a diagram will make answering the question a lot easier. Remember to keep the solution to every problem as simple as possible.

Using the SAT Math Problem Completion Process

To show you how the SAT Math process works, we'll go through an SAT Math section from *The Official SAT Study Guide For the New SAT.* We'll choose a section that includes both Multiple Choice problems and Student-Produced Response problems.

Question 1, page 407

Our diagram for this one will just be the equation as it's given in the problem. The problem is asking us to find the number that *x* represents.

As will often happen on an SAT Math question, there are two ways to solve this one—a fast way and a slow way.

The slow way is to solve the problem in the traditional algebraic way, where we would combine like terms on each side, isolate the variable, and so on.

The fast way is just to notice that every time *x* appears somewhere on one side of the equation, the number 5 appears in the same place on the other side of the equation. Since the rest of both sides of the equation are exactly the same, we know that *x* has to be equal to 5, so the answer here is (E).

As for wrong answer patterns, notice that (D) follows Hidden Pattern 1 because it's half of the correct answer.

Do you see how this isn't the sort of math question that would appear on a test in your high school math class?

Question 2, page 407

For this question, our "diagram" might be a version of the triangle that's drawn closer to scale, and with the number 3 in place of the *x*.

The question asks us to find the hypotenuse of a given right triangle when we already have two sides.

As you may remember from the toolbox, we can use the Pythagorean Theorem to find the hypotenuse of a right triangle, because we know the length of the hypotenuse is the square root of the sum of the squares of the two shorter sides.

So for this question, $y = \sqrt{(3^2 + 2^2)}$. Solve that and you'll see that $y = \sqrt{13}$. That makes (A) the answer.

The wrong answers here don't follow any particular patterns, but it's worth pointing out that (B) is what you would get if you *multiplied* the lengths of the bases instead of adding their squares, and (E) would be the length of *y* if the diagram were drawn to scale, which it isn't.

There, two questions down. That wasn't so bad, was it? Let's turn the page and keep going . . .

Question 3, page 408

My diagram for this question will be the list of factors for each answer choice.

This question wants us to find the answer choice that would be divisible by 2 and 6 but not by 4. The easiest way to do this is probably just to list all the factors for each answer choice and see where that gets us.

(A) has factors 1, 2, and 4.
(B) has factors 1, 2, 4, and 8.

(C) has factors 1, 2, 3, 4, 6, and 12.
(D) has factors 1, 2, 3, 6, 9, and 18.
(E) has factors 1, 2, 3, 4, 6, 12, and 24.

Now all we have to do is look at these lists of factors and see which one includes 2 and 6 but not 4. That's (D), so (D) is the answer.

 IMPORTANT! Notice that the solution to this question is actually very simple, once we figure out what we're being asked. This type of question would almost never appear on a high school math test, because—as we keep repeating—the SAT is not a normal math test. It's a logic test!

Question 4, page 408

My diagram for this would just be another copy of the given diagram.

The question is asking us to find the area of the circle, even though there are no numbers given in the diagram.

At this point, a lot of students will get worried because they think there's no way to solve the problem without knowing any of the dimensions of the circle. But remember that the SAT ALWAYS gives you all the information you need to figure out EVERY question with complete certainty.

So the question here is how we're going to use the given information, combined with the concepts from our toolbox, to find the answer to this problem.

Let's follow our Math problem completion process and add information into the diagram—that's always a good place to start. We know that the drawing is to scale because there's nothing telling us it's NOT to scale. We also know that the rectangle is 8-by-12. If that's true, then it must be that the short side is 8 units long and the long side is 12 units long. Let's add those measurements into our diagram.

Wait! Now we know something about the dimensions of the circle—we know that it's tangent to BC and AD, and we know that the distance from A to B and from C to D is 8 units.

That means that the diameter of the circle is 8 units. Since the diameter is twice the radius, we know the radius must be 4 units.

If you don't remember the formula for the area of a circle, all you have to do is look at the information box that appears at the beginning of every SAT Math section. It tells you the formula is $A = \pi r^2$. So that makes our area equal to 16π, and the answer is (A).

Let's check out some of our other answer choices to see how the SAT was hoping to trick us.

(B) is the answer you get if you add the lengths of the sides of the rectangle.
(C) is the answer you get if you mistakenly label the *short* side of the
    rectangle as 12 units long.
(D) is the answer you get if you calculate the area by squaring the *diameter* of the
    circle instead of the *radius*.
(E) is the area of the rectangle.

Question 5, page 408

This question, like most SAT Math questions, looks more complicated than it is. Don't let it intimidate you! Remember that the SAT can only test you on applying the concepts in the toolbox.

My diagram for this one is going to be a rough chart showing the possible outcomes of the spins.

The question is asking us to figure out the probability of obtaining a fraction that's greater than 1. This is going to involve several concepts from our toolbox:

- We have to remember that a fraction is greater than 1 when its numerator is greater than its denominator.
- We have to remember that we need to know two things in order to find the probability of an event: the number of possible outcomes, and the number of outcomes that satisfy the requirements of the event.
- We have to remember that the probability of two successive events is the product of the probabilities of each individual event.

Okay, let's get started with this. First we'll figure out the total number of possible outcomes when a 6-piece spinner is spun two times in a row. Well, we know there are 6 possible outcomes for each spin, and 6 * 6 is 36. That means there are 36 possible outcomes here. (If you couldn't determine that on your own, don't worry—the fact that each answer choice has a 36 in the denominator is a pretty good indication.)

So there are 36 possible outcomes. How many will satisfy the requirement of having the first spin be greater than the second spin?

As always, there are two ways to figure this out—a fast way and a slow way. We'll get to the fast way in a minute.

The slow way is to start with a first spin of 1 and count the total number of satisfactory outcomes given that first spin. (There are zero—if the first spin is 1, then the only possible outcomes are 1/1, 1/2, 1/3, 1/4, 1/5, and 1/6, none of which are greater than 1.)

Then we imagine a first spin of 2. With a first spin of 2, there is only one possible satisfactory outcome—2/1. The other outcomes (2/2, 2/3, 2/4, 2/5, 2/6) are all less than or equal to 1.

And we could continue like this through all 6 possible first spins, counting the satisfactory outcomes as we went. That's the slow way (though, if you were quick about it, you could still do this in a lot less than 30 seconds.)

So what's the fast way? The fast way requires you to recognize something right away. If you spin the spinner twice, calling the first spin *a* and the second spin *b*, there are three possible results:

- $a = b$
- $a < b$
- $a > b$

We're only interested in the results where $a > b$. Well, we know that there are six possible outcomes where *a* and *b* are equal (1/1, 2/2, 3/3, 4/4, 5/5, 6/6). Those are no use to us, so we can subtract them from our 36 possible outcomes. That leaves us with 30 outcomes to consider—the ones where $a > b$ or $a < b$.

Now, we also know that for every pair of spins where $a > b$, there's a corresponding pair of spins where $a < b$. In other words, for every outcome like 3/2 where $a > b$, there's an opposite outcome like 2/3 where $a < b$.

That means, of course, that the remaining 30 possible outcomes are divided evenly into satisfactory outcome and non-satisfactory outcomes—half of them will work and the other half won't.

Half of the 30 remaining outcomes is 15 possible outcomes, so the answer is (A).

Now let's look at some of the other answer choices.

(C) is what we get if we forget to take out the 6 outcomes where a and b are equal before we divide the possible outcomes in half.

(E) is what we get if we follow the solutions described above but accidentally count the *wrong* outcomes—the ones where $a \leq b$.

Don't beat yourself up if it would have taken you longer than 30 seconds to solve this problem! The test gives you over a minute per question, and with all the time you would save on other questions, you would certainly have enough time to do this problem, no matter which approach you used. The important thing to remember here is that there is *always* a fast way to do each problem—nobody catches all the shortcuts, but you should still look for them.

Question 6, page 409

Our diagram for this question will just be the charts that are already given.

This question is asking us to find the answer choice where w and x are in direct proportion.

Basically, all we're being asked is whether we know what direct proportionality is. Remember our toolbox? Direct proportionality exists between w and x when you can multiply a constant number by w and get the corresponding value for x every time.

So which answer choice allows us to do that? Only (D), where every value in column w has a corresponding value in column x that is 3 times column w. This one was pretty straightforward—on to the next!

Question 7, page 409

Sometimes students get worried when they see one of these problems that asks them to create a formula. But if we follow our process, we'll see there's no need for concern.

My diagram here is just going to be the scratch work I do as I put the formula together.

The question is asking us to put together a formula that will tell us how long it will take Dwayne to save $1,000.

We know that he pays 1/3 of his money for newspapers. If that's how much he pays out, then how much does he keep? He keeps the rest, which is 2/3 of his money. So we know that, every day, Dwayne saves $(2/3)k$. Now, if that's how much he saves in a day, how long will it take him to reach $1,000? It will take him whatever 1,000 divided by $(2/3)k$ is.

That might sound a little complicated, so let's explain it a different way. If he wanted to save $15 and he was putting away $3 every day, how long would it take him? 5 days—you can probably do that in your head. How did you do it, though? You just divided the target amount by the amount saved each day, and the result is the number of days until you hit your target.

www.grammatix.com

In our example, the target amount is 1,000, and the amount saved every day is (2/3)*k*.

So our formula will be 1,000/(2/3)*k*. But there's a problem—none of the answer choices look like that.

This is because the SAT usually gives answers in their simplest form, and we can still simplify 1,000/(2/3)*k*. How do we do that? We'll divide 1,000 by 2/3. That gives us 1,500, so the simplified version of our formula is 1,500/k, or (D).

Can you figure out what you would have to do wrong to arrive at the other answer choices?

Question 8, page 409

Our diagram for this question is going to be the multiplying we do to solve the problem.

The problem is asking us to find the spot on the number line that represents the product of the values of points *P* and *Q*. There are a couple of ways to do this. First, we could try thinking about it abstractly, and we would see that the product of a negative number with an absolute value less than 1 and a positive number between 1 and 2 would have to be a negative number with an absolute value between the absolute values of the two original numbers. But that's probably a little complicated.

What's an easier way? Remember that the number line has to be drawn to scale, since the SAT didn't tell us it was not to scale. That means we can eyeball the exact values of *P* and *Q*. *P* looks like it's equal to -.5, and *Q* is equal to 1.75. So all we have to do is multiply those, and we see that *P* * *Q* = -.875. Now we find the answer choice that represents -.875 on the number line, and we see that it's (B).

Remember—there's always a fast, simple way to do things!

Question 9, page 410

The best "diagram" here is just the solution to the given system of equations.

The question is asking us to solve the system of equations for *y*.

The easiest way to solve this is just to substitute the value given for *x* in the second equation into the first equation, which would give us

$$5y + 2(y + 1) = 23.$$

Then we simply solve for *y*, and we see that *y* = 3.

IMPORTANT! Don't make the mistake of solving for *x*! Remember that you always have to answer the question asked of you.

Question 10, page 410

The diagram for this problem will just be the calculations necessary to solve the problem.

This question is simply asking us for the value of 150% of 300. That's pretty straightforward.

If 300 appliances represent 100% of the first week, then what would be 50% of that amount? Half of 300, which is 150.

www.grammatix.com

So if the second week saw a 50% increase, then during the second week the number of appliances produced must have been 300 + 150, or 450.

Question 11, page 411

For this question, my diagram would be a drawing of the missing triangle *XYZ*, which would look exactly like *ABC* except for the lengths of its sides.

The question wants us to find one possible perimeter of *XYZ*.

A couple of concepts from the toolbox are useful here. First, recall that the perimeter of a triangle is the sum of the lengths of its sides. Also, remember that when two triangles have the same angle measurements, then the relationship between the lengths of any two corresponding sides is the same.

So in this case, if one side of *XYZ* is 24, we could say that this side corresponds to side *AB* in the given triangle. If it does, then every side in *XYZ* is 8 times as large as its corresponding side in *ABC*, because 24 is 8 times larger than 3. That would mean that the other two sides of *XYZ* would be 32 and 48 (4 * 8 and 6 * 8). If that's the case, then the perimeter is 24 + 32 + 48, or 104. So one possible answer is 104.

Notice that the question tells us there are other possible perimeters of *XYZ*. How can that be? Well, the question doesn't tell us *which* side of *XYZ* is 24. We just assumed that it was the side corresponding to side *AB*, but it could have been the one corresponding to *BC* or *CA*. Remember that Student-Produced Response questions often ask you for one correct answer out of a set of possible answers.

Question 12, page 411

Our "diagram" for this problem will be the algebraic equation we set up to answer it.

The question asks us to find the greatest of five consecutive integers whose sum is 1,000.

This is a pretty straightforward equation. If we have five consecutive integers, we can express them as x, $x + 1$, $x + 2$, $x + 3$, and $x + 4$. We want all of them together to equal 1,000, so we set up the equation like this:

$$x + (x + 1) + (x + 2) + (x + 3) + (x + 4) = 1,000$$

Once we solve that, we see that $x = 198$.

Be careful here! The question didn't ask you to find x! It asked you to find the greatest integer of the five consecutive integers, which is $x + 4$. That means the answer here is 202.

Question 13, page 411

For this question, we can probably use the given diagram, making marks on it as we need to.

The question asks us to find the value of $h(1)$, given a certain function $h(x)$ which relies on another function, $g(x)$. Remembering what the toolbox says about function notation—and remembering that SAT math always looks more complicated than it actually is—let's get started!

We're asked to find $h(1)$. To do that, we sub in the value 1 wherever x appears in the given function $h(x)$. That leaves us with

$h(1) = g(2(1)) + 2$, which we can simplify to
$h(1) = g(2) + 2$

Now we need to know what $g(2)$ is, so we can plug this value in and solve for $h(1)$. Looking at the given diagram, and remembering that it must be drawn to scale because we aren't told that it isn't, we find the value for $g(x)$ where $x = 2$. We see that this value is 1. So we put 1 in for $g(2)$, and get this:

$h(1) = 1 + 2$

Simplifying that will show us that $h(1) = 3$, so the answer is 3. That wasn't so bad, was it?

Question 14, page 411

My diagram for this one might be 4 slots representing the 4 parts, with the letters *A, B, C, D* underneath each slot. Nothing fancy. In fact, a lot of people wouldn't even diagram this one, except to work the calculation.

This is a "counting problem" from the toolbox. It's asking us to find the total number of ways that something could happen. Remember that we do this by finding the total number of possible outcomes for each mini-event, then multiplying these together. The mini-events in this situation will be the assignment of each individual part.

The first assignment can take place in any of 4 ways—any of the 4 actors could be given the part.

The second assignment can only take place in 3 ways. Why? Because one actor has already been assigned to the first part, so there are only three actors left for the second one.

The third assignment can only take place in 2 ways, for the same reason—2 actors are already taken.

Finally, the fourth assignment can only go to one actor.

So the product of the outcomes for all the mini-events is 4 * 3 * 2 * 1 = 24, and there are 24 possible ways to cast the actors.

Of course, if you're not comfortable with that, you could just list the possible outcomes and then count them. Make sure to be systematic about it, though, or you'll come up with the wrong result! Here's what it might look like if you did that:

ABCD	BACD	CABD	DABC
ABDC	BADC	CADB	DACB
ACBD	BCAD	CBAD	DBAC
ACDB	BCDA	CBDA	DBCA
ADBC	BDAC	CDAB	DCAB
ADCB	BDCA	CDBA	DCBA

Question 15, page 412

For this problem, we can basically copy the given diagram, adding our own information.

The question is asking us for the value of y, which is the measurement of an angle in the diagram.

The fastest way to solve this is basically to connect some concepts from the toolbox. We know that all the angles in an equilateral triangle are 60°, so we can label angle *QPR* accordingly. We also know that opposite angles have the same measures, so we know that angles *SPT* and *VPR* are the same size.

Now what? Well, we know that angle *QPR* has been subdivided into three equal angles, and we know that angle *VPR* includes exactly two of these subdivided angles. Each of those subdivided angles has to be 20°, since 3 of them together are 60°. That means that angle *VPR*, which includes two 20° angles, must be 40°. And since angle *VPR* is 40°, then *y* must be 40.

Question 16, page 412

Our diagram here will be the algebraic work we do to find the solution.

The problem is asking us to find the value of *y* by using a couple of made-up functions.

We begin by substituting the proper values in for *a* and *b* on both sides, and get this:

$$(4) + 3(5y) = (5y) + 4(4)$$

Then we simply combine like terms, isolate the variable, and solve, giving us

$$y = 6/5.$$

Remember that SAT Math is never as complicated as it looks!

Question 17, page 412

This problem, like so many others, probably looks harder than it is at first. There are a few ways to solve it—let's take the most straightforward one, which will still take a lot less than 30 seconds.

Some people might start in by diagramming the curve right away. You could do that, but I don't think you need to—instead, let the "diagram" be the work you do to answer the question.

Remember, from the toolbox, that the slope of a line is a fraction where the numerator is the vertical separation between two points and the denominator is the horizontal separation between those two points.

That means we're going to need two points, right? To find our two points, we'll evaluate the given equation at the given sets of points to fill in *p* and *t*.

Our first coordinate pair is (0, *p*), which means we need to find the *y* value when *x* is 0 in order to find *p*. To do that, we plug 0 in for *x* and solve:

$$(0) = y^2 - 4$$

Once we do that, we can see that *y* must be 2 or -2. (Remember that both 2 and -2 can be squared to get 4!) So the first point is either (0, -2) or (0, 2).

For the second point, we plug in 5 for *x* and solve:

$$(5) = y^2 - 4$$

When we solve, we see that *y* for this point must be either 3 or -3. So the second point is either (5, 3) or (5, -3).

Now we just need to find the greatest possible slope among those four points. Some students might figure out all four slopes (from each of the possible first points to each of the possible second points), but that will take a little more time than I feel like spending. So how can we figure out right away which slope will be the greatest?

Remember that the vertical separation goes in the numerator of the slope, and the horizontal separation goes in the denominator of the slope. Also, remember that a fraction gets bigger as its numerator gets bigger.

www.grammatix.com

Since we want the biggest possible fraction for the slope in this problem, we'll pick the two values for p and t that give us the greatest possible vertical separation, since that will give us the greatest possible numerator as well. (We don't have to worry about the denominator because the denominator represents the horizontal separation, which must be 5 since the x values of our two points can't be changed.)

The two values that give us the greatest vertical separation are -2 for p and 3 for t, which give us a vertical separation of 5.

So now we know the numerator of our slope fraction, and we also know (as previously mentioned) that the denominator has to be 5. That makes our slope fraction 5/5, or 1.

Question 18, page 412

Our "diagram" for this question is going to be the work we do in setting up and solving the equation.

The question is asking us to find the distance from Esther's house to her work place.

This might look a little tricky at first, but remember that the SAT always gives us all the information we need to solve each problem!

Let's start with what we know, and use that to see what we can figure out. We know that Esther drives 3/2 as fast in the morning as she does in the evening, because 45 is 3/2 of 30. We also know that she covers the same distance at both times of day.

Now let's think. If she covers the same distance in the evening while driving only 2/3 as fast, then we know that in the evening she must drive for 3/2 as much time.

Now we're starting to get somewhere. We know that she drove for an hour in total, and now we know that she must have driven for 3/2 as much time in the evening as she did in the morning, since she was only going 2/3 as fast in the evening.

So let's set up an equation to see how long she was driving in the morning, using t as the number of minutes:

$$t + (3/2)t = 60$$

If we solve that, we see that t equals 24.

That means Esther drove for 24 minutes in the morning, which means she must have driven for 36 minutes in the evening. Now we can take either one of those drive times and multiply it by its respective speed, and we'll know the distance that Esther drove.

There's just one small problem—we have the speed Esther drove in miles per hour, but the time she drove in minutes. So we'll need to convert the time to fractions of an hour, and then everything should be okay.

24/60 represents the portion of the hour that Esther spent driving at 45 miles per hour. We can simplify that and determine that Esther spent 2/5 of the hour doing 45. If we multiply 45 by 2/5, we see that she traveled 18 miles during those 24 minutes.

That means, finally, that the distance between Esther's workplace and her home is 18 miles.

This is probably the most complicated SAT math problem you'll ever see, but it's still nowhere near as bad as what you'd see in an advanced high school math class. Always remember two things: The SAT always gives you enough information to solve everything, and the difficult part of the solution is always the setup.

---

www.grammatix.com

Conclusion

We've just completed an entire SAT Math section, and we never really broke a sweat! We did this by sticking to our simple process, and by looking for quick and easy answers. As we saw, the hardest part of each problem was the setup. The actual calculations didn't present much of a problem, as long as we had our toolbox concepts in order.

Grammatix, Inc.

presents

how to attack

SAT Writing Multiple-Choice Questions

like a natural test-taker

These 3 Question-Type Guides will through the SAT Writing Multiple-Choice Questions quickly and easily, teaching you only what you need to know to attack these questions systematically.

www.grammatix.com

General Overview Of SAT Writing Multiple-Choice Questions

The remaining three SAT question types are all part of the Writing Section of the SAT. We'll get into the specifics of each question type in a minute, but first we need to build up an SAT Writing Toolbox just like we built up our SAT Math Toolbox.

Let's get started!

Writing Section Review: Building the SAT Writing Toolbox

The multiple-choice questions on the SAT Writing Section test a surprisingly limited number of concepts over and over again, and these concepts can be learned pretty quickly. Still, many SAT-takers are intimidated by these questions because very few of them have ever studied grammar, usage, or writing style in high school.

Before we can talk about the hidden rules and patterns of the SAT Writing Section—before we can talk about real strategy, in other words—we have to lay down some basic ideas that will form the foundation for a successful approach to this part of the SAT.

Even if you think you have a good grasp of grammar and usage, you should probably read through this section at least twice—it will only take a few minutes, and you might find that you were misinformed about something.

 What you're about to learn is NOT regular grammar! It's only enough information to get you through every real SAT Writing Question. If something seems a little strange at first, just go with it—you'll see that this simplified approach allows you to prepare quickly and easily.

All The SAT Writing Concepts You Need to Know

The concepts you need to know for the SAT Writing Section can be divided into two main groups: underlying grammatical ideas that do NOT appear on the test, and the higher-level concepts built on those ideas.

For this discussion, we'll start with the underlying ideas and move on to the higher-level concepts quickly. (I would much rather skip the underlying ideas altogether, since they don't actually appear on the SAT, but many of the higher-level concepts won't make sense without them.)

Underlying Grammatical Ideas

These basic ideas explain the essential foundation of written English as it appears on the SAT Writing Section. You'll probably find that you're familiar with most of this material, but there's a good chance you'll find some things you didn't know in here.

Parts Of Speech And Their Roles

Written English has nouns, verbs, adjectives, and conjunctions, among other things. Knowing how to identify these parts of speech, and knowing how they interact with each other, will make it possible to understand the concepts that are tested on the SAT Writing Section.

www.grammatix.com

Nouns

Nouns are the first parts of speech that babies learn, because nouns are the things you can point to. A baby can point to its mother and say, "mommy," because the word *mommy* describes an actual, physical thing. The most basic nouns are things you can point at like a baby would.

Examples: *desk, computer, pillow, food*, and *airplane* are all nouns like this.

But there are other types of nouns as well. Some nouns represent ideas, like *happiness* or *fatalism*. These nouns are things that you can't point at. But don't worry—you can usually recognize them by their endings.

Examples: If a word ends in *–ness, -ism, -hood, -ology*, or anything similar, it's probably a noun.

Nouns can be either singular or plural. The plural form of a noun is usually formed with the suffix *–s* or the suffix *–es*, but there are some special nouns that form their plurals differently.

Examples: *shoe, box,* and *mouse* are all singular nouns, and *shoes, boxes,* and *mice* are the plural forms of those nouns.

Pronouns are a special sub-set of nouns. A pronoun is a word that shows us we're dealing with a noun we've already talked about. Usually, pronouns take the place of the nouns they refer to.

Examples: *I, you, he, she, it, we, they, me, you, him, her, us, them, one, which,* and *that* are all pronouns. When we have a sentence like *Thomas wants to know why he has to do the dishes*, the *he* lets us know that we're still talking about the same person. It would sound strange to say *Thomas wants to know why Thomas has to do the dishes*, so we use the pronoun *he* in place of the second *Thomas*.

On the SAT Writing Section, a pronoun must always be used in a way that clearly indicates which noun (or nouns) it replaces.

Example: This is a good sentence on the SAT:

Amy and Elizabeth were playing cards with Billy when Amy became angry with him.

- *him* is pronoun that clearly refers to the noun *Billy*, which appears earlier in the sentence.

This is a bad sentence on the SAT:

*Amy and Elizabeth were playing cards with Billy when she became angry at him.

- *she* is a pronoun that could refer either to the noun *Amy* or to the noun *Elizabeth*.

On the SAT Writing Section, you can use either *one* or *you* as a pronoun that refers to an unspecified person, but the use must be consistent within a sentence.
Examples: These are okay sentences on the SAT:

One should take care to mind one's manners.

You should take care to mind your manners.

- *One* and *you* can both act as pronouns that refer generally to an unspecified person as long as they don't appear in the same sentence together.

This is not an okay sentence on the SAT:

*One should take care to mind your manners.

- *One* cannot be used interchangeably with *you*—the usage must be consistent for each sentence.

Subjects and objects
The common subject pronouns—pronoun forms which can appear as the subjects of verbs—are *I, you, he, she, it, we, they,* and *who.* These are the only pronoun forms that can be used as subjects, and, except for *you,* they can ONLY be used as subjects.
Examples: This is a bad sentence on the SAT:

*He gave the present to she.

- *He* is a correctly-used subject pronoun, and its verb is *gave.*
- *she* is a subject pronoun that is NOT being used as the subject of any verb.

This is an acceptable sentence on the SAT:

He gave the present to her.

- *her* is not a subject pronoun and is not the subject of a verb.

The SAT will often try to use subject pronouns where they don't belong!

Personal pronouns
When a pronoun takes the place of a noun that indicates a person, it has to be a personal pronoun.
Examples: This is a bad sentence on the SAT:

*I gave the report to the supervisor that asked me for it.

www.grammatix.com

- *supervisor* is a noun that indicates a person—supervisors are people.
- *that* is not a personal pronoun, even though it refers to the personal noun *supervisor*.

This is a good sentence on the SAT:

I gave the report to the supervisor who asked me for it.

- *who* is a personal pronoun that refers to the personal noun *supervisor*.

Verbs

Verbs are the second-most basic class of words. A verb is an action. Verbs are things you can do—the word *do* is a verb itself. Here's a test for identifying English verbs: if you can create a sentence that puts a word after word *cannot*, then that word can be a verb. Examples: *jog*, *eat*, *initiate*, and *go* can all be verbs in English; you can test this by creating sentences like *Judy cannot go to the movies*, where the word *go* is able to appear after the word *cannot*.

A verb takes different forms, called "conjugations," depending on the time period of the action the verb describes. For the purposes of the SAT, we only care about two apects of a conjugation:

- whether a verb-form is singular or plural (the verb's "number"), and
- whether a verb's action takes place in the present, past, or future (the verb's "tense")

Singular versus plural verbs:

Like nouns, verbs have singular and plural forms. Plural forms of verbs often end in –s.

Examples: In the sentence

Today we hike for the summit.

- *we* is a plural pronoun that requires a plural verb, and *hike* is a plural verb-form.

In the sentence

Today Joe hikes for the summit.

- *Joe* is a singular noun that requires a singular verb, and *hikes* is a singular verb-form.

In many cases, the singular and plural forms of a verb are identical. Examples: In the sentence

I like hiking.

- *Like* is a singular verb-form that correctly agrees with the singular pronoun *I*.

In the sentence

We like hiking.

- *We* is a plural pronoun correctly modified by the plural verb-form *like*.

A verb must always agree in number with the noun or nouns that it modifies. Examples: This is a correct sentence:

Monica and Alex enjoy the theater.

- *Monica* and *Alex* are each singular nouns.
- *enjoy* is a plural verb-form that modifies two nouns.

This sentence is incorrect:

*Monica and Alex enjoys the theater.

- *enjoys* is a singular verb-form that might seem, at first, like it correctly modifies the noun *Alex*. But in this sentence it has to modify the phrase *Monica and Alex*, which consists of two singular nouns and requires a plural verb-form.

Mixing singular verbs with plural nouns, and plural nouns with singular verbs, is a common error on the SAT Writing Section. Always check to see which noun a verb is supposed to agree with!

Tenses of verbs

As we discussed before, verbs describe actions. These actions are either going on right now, already over, or about to happen later on. We have three basic tenses to describe when the action of a verb takes place: past, present, and future.
Examples: In this sentence,

I love my grandmother.

- *love* is a present-tense verb-form, which indicates that the action of loving my grandmother is going on right now.

In this sentence,

I will love my children very much when I have them.

- *will love* is a future verb-form that indicates that the loving has not started yet.

In this sentence,

I loved my pet goldfish.

- *loved* is a past-tense verb-form, indicating that the act of loving has already finished.

There are other verb-forms that we have to be able to recognize on the SAT Writing Section, as well. It isn't necessary to know the names of these forms, but it is necessary to know whether they indicate action in the past or present. These verb-forms are the ones that use the "helping verbs" *to have* and *to be*.

For the purposes of the SAT Writing Section, all verb-forms that use any form of the helping verb *to have* indicate actions in the past.
Example: In this sentence,

I had not improved my SAT score before I stopped guessing, but I have improved it since then.

- *had not improved* indicates an action in the past, because *had* is a form of the helping verb *to have*.
- *stopped* indicates an action in the past.
- *have improved* indicates an action in the past, because *have* is a form of the helping verb *to have*.

For the purpose of the SAT Writing Section, all verb-forms that use a past-tense form of the verb *to be* indicate actions in the past.
Example: In this sentence,

I was thinking about my homework last night.

- *was thinking* indicates an action in the past, because it includes the helping verb-form *was*, which is a past-tense form of the verb *to be*.

For the purpose of the SAT Writing Section, all verb-forms that use a present-tense form of the verb *to be* indicate actions in the present.
Example: In this sentence,

I am thinking about pie for dessert.

- *am thinking* indicates an action in the present, because it involves *am*, which is a present-tense form of the helping verb *to be*.

On the SAT Writing Section, all verbs in a sentence should indicate actions in the same time frame wherever possible.
Examples: This is an okay sentence on the SAT Writing Section:

The dinner you served us was delicious.

- *served* and *was* are both verb-forms that indicate action in the past.

This sentence would not be acceptable on the SAT Writing Section:

*The dinner you served us is delicious.

- *served* is a past-tense verb-form, indicating action in the past.
- *is* is a present-tense verb-form, indicating action in the present.

The SAT Writing Section likes to test your ability to put verbs in the same tenses, so always be on the lookout when a sentence contains verbs that are in different tenses.

Conjugations of verbs

English verbs, like verbs in any other language, have specific conjugations that show their tenses. (Conjugations also show things like a verb's "mood" and "voice," but those aren't tested on the SAT Writing Section, so we won't worry about them.)
Example: In this sentence,

Mrs. Smith has decided to buy a new car.

- *has decided* is the "past participle" conjugation of the verb *to decide*.

The SAT Writing Section will occasionally show you a verb-form that is conjugated incorrectly.
Examples: This is a good sentence on the SAT:

The subject of money has arisen many times in our discussions.

- *has arisen* is a correct conjugation of the verb *to arise*.
This is a bad sentence on the SAT:

*The subject of money has arosen many times in our discussions.

- *has arosen* is not a verb-form in English; instead, it's a strange and incorrect combination of the proper past-tense form *arose* and the proper past participle *has arisen*.

Verb-forms as nouns

Two verb-forms can function as nouns. These are the *–ing* and *to* forms of verbs.

Examples: In this sentence,

Singing is a lot of fun.

- *Singing* is a form of the verb *to sing* that acts like a noun—it's the subject of the verb-form *is*.

Special verbs: *to be* and *to become*

To be and *to become* are members of a special group of verbs called "copulars." Copular verbs are verbs that show us when two things are, or will be, the same thing. (You don't need to know the term "copular" for the SAT, by the way.)

To use a copular verb properly, you place a noun phrase before it, and either another noun phrase or an adjective phrase after it.

Examples: In this sentence,

Muhammad Ali was a great boxer.

- *Muhammad Ali* is a noun phrase that is being equated to the noun phrase *a great fighter*.
- *was* is a singular, past-tense form of the copular verb *to be*, which is equating the noun phrase before it to the noun phrase after it.
- *a great boxer* is a noun phrase that is being equated to the noun phrase *Muhammad Ali*.

On the SAT Writing Section, the noun phrases on either side of a copular verb must have the same number.

Examples: This is an acceptable sentence on the SAT Writing Section:

My cousins want to become astronauts.

- *My cousins* is a plural noun phrase that is being equated to the plural noun phrase *astronauts*.
- *to become* is a copular verb.
- *astronauts* is a plural noun that is being equated to the plural noun phrase *cousins*.

This is an unacceptable sentence on the SAT Writing Section:

*My cousins want to become an astronaut.

- *My cousins* is a plural noun phrase that is being equated to the singular noun phrase *an astronaut*, which is no good on the SAT.
- *to become* is a copular verb.
- *an astronaut* is a singular noun phrase that is being improperly equated to the plural noun phrase *my cousins*.

Adjectives and adverbs

Adjectives are single words that describe nouns. An adjective usually appears immediately before its noun, or before a list of other adjectives that appears before the noun.

Example: In this sentence,

Sally ordered an Italian salad.

- *Italian* is an adjective that tells us something about the noun *salad*, and appears immediately before it.

When you want to use an adjective to modify something that is not a noun, you have to use the "adverb" form of the adjective. The adverb-form of an adjective almost always ends in *–ly*.

Example: In this sentence,

That is a very cleverly written essay.

- *cleverly* is the adverb-form of the adjective *clever*, which modifies the word *written* (note that *written* not a noun, which is why it can only be modified by an adverb).

The SAT Writing Section will often try to fool you by incorrectly using an adjective form to modify a word that is not a noun.

Examples: This is a bad sentence on the SAT:

*You have to move quick if you want a seat.

- *quick* is an adjective, but there is no noun after it, so it isn't modifying a noun and should appear as an adverb.

This is a correct sentence on the SAT:

You have to move quickly if you want a seat.

- *quickly* is an adverb that describes the verb *to move*.

Exception: adjectives with copular verbs

Remember our discussion of copular verbs like *to be* and *to become*, which equate the things on either side of them? For these special verbs, we can use adjective forms even when they don't appear immediately before nouns.

Example: This is an okay sentence on the SAT:

You have to be quick if you want a seat.

- *you* is a pronoun that is correctly modified by the adjective *quick*.

- *to be* is a copular verb that equates the word *you* with the word *quick*.
- *quick* is an adjective that does not appear before a verb but does appear after a correctly used copular verb.

Conjunctions

Conjunctions are words that link ideas to each other.

Examples: *and, either, or, neither, nor,* and *because* can all act like conjunctions on the SAT.

On the SAT, when two ideas are linked by a conjunction, the ideas must appear in the same form.

Examples: This is a good sentence on the SAT Writing Section:

Samantha likes singing, dancing, and acting.

- *singing, dancing,* and *acting* are all being linked together by the conjunction *and*, and they all appear in their *–ing* forms.

This is a bad sentence on the SAT Writing Section:

*Samantha likes singing, dancing, and to act.

- *singing, dancing,* and *to act* are all ideas linked together by the conjunction *and*, but they don't all appear in the same form—*singing* and *dancing* are in their *–ing* forms, but *to act* is in its *to* form.

Prepositions

Prepositions are words that describe the origins or relative positions of ideas in a sentence.

Example: In the sentence

The letter from your mother is in the drawer under the table.

- *from your mother* is a prepositional phrase in which the preposition *from* shows that the origin of the letter is the noun phrase *your mother*
- *in the drawer* is a prepositional phrase in which the preposition *in* shows the position of the letter relative to the drawer
- *under the table* is a prepositional phrase in which the preposition *under* shows the position of the drawer relative to the table

Prepositions are also used in certain idioms in English, and the SAT likes to test your knowledge of these idioms occasionally.

Examples: This is a bad sentence on the SAT:

*Joey's supervisor fell to love with the new idea.

- *fell to love* is an improper usage of an English idiom because the preposition *to* should be replaced with another preposition.

This is an acceptable sentence on the SAT:

Joey's supervisor fell in love with the new idea.

- *fell in love* is a proper usage of an English idiom.

Sometimes the SAT Writing Section places a prepositional phrase between a subject and its verb, and tries to trick you by making the verb agree with the noun in the prepositional phrase instead of with the actual subject.
Examples: This is an acceptable sentence on the SAT:

Andrea's list of chores is very complicated.

- *list* is the subject of the verb-form *is*.
- *of chores* is a prepositional phrase that comes between the subject *list* and the verb *is*
- *is* is a verb, so it has to be singular to match the singular noun *list*

This is not an acceptable sentence on the SAT:

*Andrea's list of chores are very complicated.

- *chores* is a plural noun, but it is NOT the subject in this sentence—the subject is *list*, and *chores* is part of a prepositional phrase that describes the subject.
- *are* is a plural verb-form that has incorrectly been made to agree with the plural noun *chores*, which is not the subject of the sentence.

Comparatives

Comparatives are phrases that compare one idea to another.
They can be formed by pairing the *–er* form of an adjective with the word *than* in order to compare two or more things. (Where necessary, comparatives can also be formed with the words *more* or *less* before an adjective instead of with that adjective's *–er* form.)
Example: In this sentence, *nicer than* is a comparative:

I think your new car is nicer than your old one.

In this sentence, *more intelligent than* is a comparative:

This solution seems more intelligent than the old approach.

Comparatives can also be formed with phrases that use the word *as* twice.

Example: In this sentence, the phrase *as interesting as* is a comparative phrase:

I don't think our calculus class is as interesting as our art class.

When you see a comparative on the SAT, make sure that the phrase that comes right after the comparative phrase really belongs in the comparison.
Examples: This is a good SAT sentence:

Your house is smaller than John's house.

- *smaller than* is the comparative phrase that compares the idea of *your house* to the idea of *John's house*.

This is a bad SAT sentence:

Your house is smaller than John.

- *John* is not what the phrase *Your house* should really be compared to; the way this sentence is written, it says that your house is smaller than a person named John.

Be on the lookout for comparatives in the SAT Writing Section! They're very often handled incorrectly

Clauses and phrases

A phrase is a group of words that serves a particular function in a sentence. Usually, this function is analogous to a part of speech.
A phrase can include one or more words.
Phrases are referred to by the functions they fulfill within their sentences. There are "noun phrases," "verb phrases," "prepositional phrases," "adverbial phrases," et cetera.
Examples: In the sentence

The cat who lives next door likes my pineapple tree.

- *The cat* is a noun phrase.
- *lives next door* is a verb phrase.
- *The cat who lives next door* is a noun phrase that includes the noun phrase *The cat* and the verb phrase *lives next door*
- *likes my pineapple tree* is a verb phrase
- *my pineapple tree* is a noun phrase.
(There are other phrases that could be said to exist in this sentence, but you get the idea.)

Don't worry if this doesn't make a lot of sense! The SAT doesn't actually test your knowledge of phrases, or your ability to pull phrases out of a sentence. We're only covering these ideas so that when I say, "the noun phrase such-and-such," you'll have some idea what I'm talking about.

A clause is a group of words that includes a subject noun phrase, a verb phrase, and, if necessary, an object noun phrase.
Example: This is a complete clause:

This pizza recipe requires cheese.

- *This pizza recipe* is the subject noun phrase.
- *requires* is the verb phrase.
- *cheese* is the object noun phrase.

A clause can be either "independent" or "dependent."
A "dependent" clause begins with a conjunction.
An "independent" clause does not begin with a conjunction.
Example: In the sentence,

You have to sleep more because you study too much.

- *You have to sleep more* is an independent clause because it has all the elements of a clause and does not start with a conjunction.
- *because you study too much* is a dependent clause because it starts with the conjunction *because*.

For the multiple-choice questions on the SAT Writing Section, every correctly written sentence must contain at least one independent clause.

Clauses and commas

Independent clauses cannot be separated from each other by a comma.
Examples: This is a bad sentence on the SAT:

*I have not yet begun to fight, time is on my side.

- *I have not yet begun to fight* is an independent clause including the subject pronoun *I* and the verb-form *have begun*.
- *time is on my side* is an independent clause including the subject noun *time* and the copular verb-form *is*.

This is an acceptable sentence on the SAT:

I have not yet begun to fight; time is on my side.

Conditionals

A "conditional" is a statement that uses the conjunction *if*. Properly written conditional sentences avoid using the word *would* in the clause that begins with *if*.
Examples: This is a bad SAT sentence:

www.grammatix.com

*I would have stopped by your house if I would have known you were home.

- *would have stopped* is acceptable because it appears in the clause *I would have stopped by*, which does not contain the word *if*.
- *if* is the conditional conjunction.
- *would have known* is incorrect here because it uses the word *would* in the same clause where the word *if* appears.

This sentence is acceptable on the SAT:

I would have stopped by your house if I had known you were home.

- *would have stopped* is acceptable because it does not appear in the same clause as the conjunction *if*.
- *if* is the conditional conjunction.

Dangling participles

A participle is a special verb-form that can end in *–ing*, *-en*, or *–ed*. They're often used at the beginning of a sentence.
Example: In this sentence,

Screaming for help, the mailman ran away from the angry dog.

- *Screaming* is a participle.

When these participles are used in standard written English, they are always understood to refer to the first noun phrase in the independent clause in the sentence.
Example: In the sentence above,

- *Screaming for help* is the participial phrase, beginning with the participle *screaming* (an *–ing* word)
- *the mailman ran away from the angry dog* is the independent clause (remember that an independent clause has a subject noun phrase and main verb phrase).

We know this participle was used correctly because the word *screaming* describes the word *mailman*, which is what we wanted to do.

This sentence, however, would be completely INCORRECT:

*Screaming for help, the dog chased the mailman down the street.

What's wrong with that? We still have a participial phrase (*screaming for help*) and an independent clause (*the dog chased the mailman down the street*), but the problem is that the participle in this sentence can't possibly describe the first noun phrase in the independent clause, which is *the dog*. This sentence is garbage because the dog can't scream. Only the mailman can scream.

Examples: In the sentence,

Encouraged by her previous successes, Martha decided to try again.

- *Encouraged by her previous successes* is the participial phrase, starting with the participle *encouraged*.
- *Martha decided to try again* is the independent clause, containing the noun phrase *Martha* and the verb phrase *decided to try again*.

Now, is this example used properly? Let's see. The way this is written, the thing that is being encouraged is Martha. Is that what we're trying to say? Yes, it is—Martha is the one who's encouraged, so this participle is used correctly. But if the sentence went this way instead,

*Encouraged by her previous successes, the future was all Martha thought about.

then we wouldn't have a good sentence anymore, because the future isn't something that can be encouraged.

Participles show up often in the SAT Writing Section, and they're almost always used incorrectly, so look out for them!

Higher-Level Concepts: Ideal Sentences And Paragraphs On The SAT

Now that we've talked about the basic underlying grammatical rules you need for the SAT Writing Section, we need to discuss the sorts of things that the SAT considers to be "good" usage. To do this, we'll talk in terms of the "bad" and "good" patterns that appear on the SAT.

On the SAT Writing Section, ideal sentences are the ones that avoid certain "bad" patterns and make us of certain "good" patterns. The fewer "bad" patterns and the more "good" patterns a sentence has, the more "SAT-ideal" the sentence is.

"Bad" patterns that often appear in errors on the SAT Writing Section.	"Good" patterns that indicate correct usage on the SAT.
-ing words Errors on the SAT Writing Section often involve -ing words that don't correctly modify nouns they refer to, or that don't belong in a sentence at all.	Use of an –ing word so that it correctly modifies the first noun phrase after the comma in the sentence is acceptable on the SAT Writing Section; otherwise, avoid –ing words whenever possible.
-ed words Errors on the SAT Writing Section often involve -ed words that don't correctly modify the nouns they refer to.	Use of an –ed word so that it correctly modifies the first noun phrase after the comma in the sentence is also acceptable on the SAT Writing Section.
pronouns Errors on the SAT Writing Section often involve the use of pronouns when they aren't needed or when they don't refer to any particular noun.	Pronouns that agree with their main nouns in number are okay. It's also okay to use either *you* or *one*, as long the usage is consistent. Finally, pronouns must clearly indicate which nouns they're replacing.
non-parallelism Errors on the SAT often involve the use of conjunctions when the ideas joined by the conjunction are not in the same form.	Words and phrases joined by conjunctions should use parallel structures.
incorrect verb-forms Conjugating verbs incorrectly is an error on the SAT.	All verb use must be consistent with normal, standard usage.
non-agreement Using a pronoun that doesn't agree in number with its noun, or a verb that doesn't agree in number with its noun or pronoun, is an error on the SAT.	All pronouns in a correctly written sentence must agree in number with their main nouns, and all verbs with their nouns or pronouns.

www.grammatix.com

"Bad" patterns that often appear in errors on the SAT Writing Section.	"Good" patterns that indicate correct usage on the SAT.
adjectives versus adverbs On the SAT, using an adjective to describe anything besides a noun is an error.	All adjectives in a correctly written sentence are used to describe nouns. Words that describe anything else appear as adverbs.
***as* in general** On the SAT, the word *as* is likely to appear in poorly written sentences.	The word *as* can appear in a correctly written SAT sentence when it is used to compare two or more things, or when it's part of a phrase that correctly modifies the first noun that appears after a comma.
verb tense On the SAT, incorrect sentences often have verbs in multiple tenses.	Correctly written sentences on the SAT either place all verb phrases in the same tense or properly signify a tense shift with a time expression like *before* or *next year*.
commas separating complete clauses Incorrectly written sentences on the SAT often use EITHER a comma OR a conjunction to separate two complete clauses.	Correctly written sentences on the SAT either separate complete clauses with a semicolon or dash, or add a conjunction like *since*, *because*, or *and* between the comma and the beginning of the second clause.
to be, to become When the verb *to be* or *to become* is the only verb in a clause, incorrectly written SAT sentences often make the nouns on either side of the verb differ in number.	Correctly written SAT sentences make the noun phrases on either side of *to be* or *to become* appear in the same number.
removing *to be* when possible Incorrectly written SAT sentences often include the verb *to be* when they don't need to.	Correctly written SAT sentences use the verb *to be* either to equate two ideas or as a helping verb for other verbs-forms.
removing *the* when possible Incorrectly written SAT sentences sometimes use *a*, *an*, and *the* when they aren't necessary.	Correctly written SAT sentences use articles to modify noun phrases only when they're needed.

www.grammatix.com

"Bad" patterns that often appear in errors on the SAT Writing Section.	"Good" patterns that indicate correct usage on the SAT.
parallelism with *than* Incorrectly written SAT sentences might use comparisons with *than* when the two things being compared don't have parallel structures.	Correctly written SAT sentences use comparisons with *than* only when the structures of the two things being compared are parallel, in order to assure that the proper things are being compared.
either/or* versus *either/and Incorrectly written SAT sentences occasionally use *and* with *either*.	When correctly written SAT sentences use the word *either*, it appears with the conjunction *or*, not *and*.
idioms—prepositions Incorrectly written SAT sentences often use the prepositions in common idioms.	Correctly written SAT sentences use the normal prepositions in everyday idioms.
proper pronoun usage (he/him) Incorrectly written SAT sentences might use subject pronouns where object pronouns should appear.	Correctly written SAT sentences use object pronouns as the objects of verbs and prepositions.
conjunctions at beginning of sentence Incorrectly written SAT sentences often begin with conjunctions even though there are no independent clauses in the sentence.	Correctly written SAT sentences only begin with conjunctions when they include independent clauses.
if* and *would have Incorrect SAT sentences use *would have* instead of *had* immediately after *if*.	Correctly written SAT sentences use *had* in *if* phrases, not *would have*.
removing *which* when possible Incorrectly written SAT sentences use *which* when they don't need to.	Correctly written SAT sentences avoid *which* whenever possible.
relative pronouns—personal with people Incorrect SAT sentences use impersonal pronouns to take the place of personal nouns.	Correctly written SAT sentences use personal pronouns to replace personal nouns.
comparatives Incorrectly written SAT sentences use both *more* and *–er* to form comparatives.	Correctly written SAT sentences use either *more* or the suffix *–er*—not both—to form comparatives.
redundancy Incorrectly written SAT sentences might express the same idea twice.	Correctly written SAT sentences avoid redundancy by expressing each idea only once.
avoiding conjunctions Incorrectly written SAT sentences might use conjunctions where they aren't necessary.	Correctly written SAT sentences only use conjunctions when necessary, and use them to link ideas appropriately.

www.grammatix.com

About Paragraphs

Ideal paragraphs on the SAT are paragraphs that contain as few concepts as possible.

When adding a sentence to a paragraph in the Improving Paragraphs portion of the SAT Writing Section, add the sentence that contains the fewest concepts that are not already in the paragraph.

When removing sentences from paragraphs in the Improving Paragraphs portion of the SAT Writing Section, remove sentences that introduce concepts that do not appear elsewhere in the paragraph.

General Overview of Improving Sentences on the SAT Writing Section

The Improving Sentences questions on the SAT Writing Section are relatively straightforward and repetitive once you've mastered the concepts in the Writing Toolbox. Each question presents you with a sentence that has an underlined word or phrase. The answer choices then provide you with several possible versions of the underlined portion of the prompt sentence. Your job is to choose the version of the underlined phrase that fits best.

Don't worry! You'll find that these questions test a fairly limited number of concepts, and—like everything else on the SAT—you'll be able to answer them pretty mechanically with a little practice. Let's get started.

www.grammatix.com

The Rules for Improving Sentences on the SAT

We don't need to talk about that many rules for these questions, because there's very little variation from question to question. Here are the 3 rules you'll need.

SAT Improving Sentences Rule 1: Style Counts

Sometimes the difference between a wrong answer choice and a correct answer choice is a question of style, not grammar. Sometimes, according to the SAT, one of the answer choices just "feels" better.

This might upset you at first—how are you supposed to know what the SAT thinks is good writing style? Don't worry. In the SAT Writing Toolbox, we've broken down all the patterns that appear in bad SAT answers and contrasted them with the patterns that appear in good answers. That way, instead of worrying about "style," all you have to do is avoid the answer choices with bad patterns and choose the one with the greatest number of good patterns.

SAT Improving Sentences Rule 2: Don't Make Trouble

The correct answer choice must not only fix any mistake in the underlined portion of the prompt sentence—it also has to avoid creating new mistakes.

Sometimes students zero-in on a problem in the prompt sentence and then choose the first answer choice that gets rid of that particular problem. But this isn't good enough! The correct answer choice must not have ANY mistakes.

SAT Improving Sentences Rule 3: (A) Is The Same

This isn't really worth mentioning from a strategic perspective, but it's probably still worth pointing out—the first answer choice in each Improving Sentences question is an exact restatement of the underlined portion of the prompt sentence.

This won't really affect the right answer at all, because we still want to find the answer choice that avoids the bad patterns from the Toolbox and includes the good ones. But we thought we should mention it just in case, because some students skip the instructions to each section and get confused when they can't see a difference between the prompt sentence and choice (A).

The Hidden Pattern of Improving Sentences on the SAT

The major hidden grammatical patterns of all SAT Writing Multiple Choice Sections are already covered in the Toolbox. The hidden pattern in this section pertains only to answer choices for the Improving Sentences questions.

Hidden Pattern 1: The Shortest Answer is Often Best

The correct answer choice for SAT Improving Sentences questions is very often the shortest answer choice. This is because the best way to fix the kinds of errors that appear on the Improving Sentences questions is usually to cut things out.

When the correct answer choice is NOT the shortest one, it's very often the longest one. This is because the other common way to fix the kinds of errors that appear in this section is to add words and phrases.

This is NOT the same thing as saying that you should always pick the shortest or longest answer. That would be idiotic. All we're trying to say is that the correct answer is very often the shortest or longest answer choice. Knowing this helps us start to take apart the Improving Sentences questions, because it calls our attention to the fact that the best solutions to these questions often involve cutting as much as possible from, or adding as much as possible to, the given sentence.

The SAT Improving Sentences Process

Here is the process I recommend for SAT Improving Sentences Questions.

1. Read the entire prompt sentence.

The first step in attacking these questions is to read the entire sentence, since you need to know the context of each element in the sentence.

2. Look for a pattern in the sentence that the SAT likes to avoid.

The next thing to do is to look for patterns the SAT Writing Section likes to avoid. For these, look back at the chart of "bad" and "good" patterns. We'll scan for each one individually: *-ing* words, *–ed* words, pronouns, conjunctions, prepositions, non-parallelism, et cetera.

`[If you find one or more of these patterns, proceed to step 3.]`

`[If you don't find any of these patterns, proceed to step 8.]`

3. Focus only on the underlined portion of the sentence.

Remember the rules for this section—we can only change things that are underlined, and we can only change them in the ways that appear in the answer choices! You have to focus on the underlined portion of the sentence. Without trying to rewrite it on your own, think about how the patterns you identified in step 2 affect the underlined portion of the sentence.

4. Read the shortest answer choice out of choices (B), (C), (D), and (E).

The SAT is big on simplicity when it comes to multiple-choice Writing questions, which means that the shortest answer choice is often (but NOT ALWAYS!) the correct one. So, with the underlined portion of the sentence in mind, find the shortest answer choice and consider it first; look for it to eliminate as many "bad" patterns as possible, without introducing new ones. Whether you think it's the correct choice or not, go on to the next step—you NEVER mark an answer on the SAT without at least reading all the other choices!

5. Read the longest answer choice from choices (B), (C), (D), and (E).

If the underlined portion of the prompt sentence was missing something, then the correct answer choice may well be the longest one, because it adds the most to the prompt sentence. We consider this answer choice after the shortest one because, generally speaking, it's the second-most likely to be correct after the shortest one. (This does NOT mean that the longest answer MUST be correct if the shortest answer is incorrect. The correct answer is correct because it is grammatically sound, not because of its length.)

There's another reason that we read the shortest answer choice first and the longest answer choice second. Because of the way the SAT structures its answer choices, reading these two answer choices first will give us an idea of the "range" of possible answer choices. If we think the ideal answer choice would be shorter than the shortest answer choice or longer than the longest one, there's a good chance we misunderstood something somewhere, and we should either skip the question or start over.

6. Read all other answer choices.

Once we've read the shortest answer choice and the longest answer choice, we read the other three. Remember—you never answer an SAT question without reading all the answer choices, even if you think the shortest or longest answer choice is correct.

7. Weigh the benefits of each choice to find the most "SAT-ideal" choice.

Remember the patterns that the SAT likes to avoid, and the patterns it likes to use—we talked about all of these in the SAT Writing Toolbox. The correct answer choice to each question is the one that minimizes the number of "bad" patterns in the sentence and maximizes the number of "good" patterns. In other words, the correct answer choice is the one that optimizes the prompt sentence so that it comes as close as possible to an ideal SAT Writing sentence.

When you've done that, go on to Step 8 to take a final look at choice (A).

8. Consider that there might be nothing wrong with the sentence.

Remember that there might not be an answer choice that makes the sentence any more "SAT-ideal" than the version presented in the prompt. If this is the case, then the correct answer is (A).

Don't forget that the answer choice distribution for SAT Writing questions is the same as it is for any other multiple-choice SAT question type. Choice (A) can be correct as frequently (or as infrequently) as any other answer choice.

```
[If you're certain that one answer choice avoids more "bad"
patterns and incorporates more "good" patterns than the other
four, choose it and move on to the next question.]
```

```
[If you aren't certain which answer choice is best, skip the
question.  Consider coming back to it if you have time later.]
```

SAT Improving Sentences Process Conclusion

We've now seen the entire process for Improving Sentences questions on the SAT Writing Section. In the next section, we'll show you the process in action against real SAT questions published by the College Board!

Using the SAT Writing Process to Improve Sentences

To prove that the SAT Writing Process will show you how to find sentence errors, we'll go through all the Identifying Sentence Errors Questions in section 7 of the first sample SAT that appears in the College Board publication *The Official SAT Study Guide For the New SAT*.

Question 1, page 413

This is an example of a sentence that is grammatically acceptable but stylistically bad. Remember that you'll see a lot of sentences like this on the Writing section of the SAT.

Choice (E) does a lot of things that we look for the right answer to do. It gets rid of the words *by*, *that*, and *and*, which appear in the other answer choices. It's also the shortest answer choice, which is another strong indication that it's the right answer.

Note that every single answer choice would be grammatically acceptable—always remember that the Improving Sentences questions are often more a test of writing style than of grammatical correctness.

Question 2, page 413

In this question, we see a phrase that begins with a word that ends in *–ed*, so we know we have to be careful about what it's modifying. Is *Sarah's search* actually carrying the luggage? Of course not—a search can't carry anything. The only answer choice that starts with a word that can actually be "burdened" with something is (E), which starts with the word *Sarah*.

You should also notice right away that (E) is the shortest answer, something we often see in the correct answer choice.

Finally, when you look at the other answer choices, you'll see that they're full of words like *what* and *which*, which are pronouns we want to avoid whenever possible.

Question 3, page 413

This question has a pronoun in the underlined portion that could refer to either of two people in the non-underlined portion. We know that the SAT Writing Section doesn't like pronouns to be used carelessly, so we should look for an answer choice that makes things clear by changing the pronoun to a regular noun. That leaves us with (C), (D). and (E), which replace *he* with *Sam*.

Of those three answer choices, (D) and (E) use conjunctions like *since* and *and*, while (C) avoids these. That makes (C) the more attractive choice according to the hidden patterns of the SAT Writing Section, so it's the right answer.

Question 4, page 413

For this question, we see once again that the shortest answer is the correct one. Although (D) does have the word *that*, which we try to avoid in the correct answer, other answer choices have *because* and *as*, and are also longer. That makes (D) the most

---

www.grammatix.com

attractive answer according to the hidden rules and patterns of the SAT Writing Section. (Remember, too, that we can't separate independent clauses with commas.)

Question 5, page 413

This question has one of our parallel structures in it! Remember that whenever we see a phrase with a conjunction that we can't get rid of—like *not only x, but y*—we want *x* and *y* to be as structurally similar as possible. Notice that *x* in this sentence starts with *by the*, and *y* starts with *it has*. That's not good!

The only answer choice that also has *by the* is (C), which is the correct answer.

Question 6, page 414

For this question, every answer choice but (A) adds an extra word that ends in *–ing*, something the SAT Writing Section strongly dislikes. The correct choice is the only one that doesn't do this, (A).

Question 7, page 414

This one is a little tricky! Remember that the SAT Writing Section often makes the shortest answer the correct answer. Here, though, the two shortest answers both involve the word *they*, which is a pronoun. We know the SAT Writing Section doesn't like to use pronouns when we don't know which words the pronouns are replacing—in this sentence, there is no mention of who *they* refers to.

In fact, the only two answer choices that get rid of *they* are (C) and (D), which talk about *the linguist* instead. (C) uses a conjunction without a comma to join two independent clauses, so (D) is the right answer.

 Note that, in this case, the correct answer choice is the LONGEST one, not the shortest one, and it also includes the word *which*, which is something the SAT doesn't usually like. Remember that, for every question, you have to weigh the "bad" patterns against the "good" ones to determine the correct answer.

Question 8, page 414

For this question, (C) and (D) both use the wrong form of the verb *provide*—(C) messes up because it introduces an *–ing* word, and (D) tries to confuse you into thinking that *animals* is the word doing the providing, when really it's *observation*.

That leaves us with (A), (B), and (E) as the answer choices that get the verb right. (B) is a bad comparison because it compares *sustained observation* to *many animals*. (E) is a bad choice because it begins with a prepositional phrase that isn't set off by commas on both sides. That leaves only (A) as the correct choice.

Question 9, page 414

For this one, we want an answer choice that gets rid of the *–ing* word in the underlined portion of the prompt. That eliminates choices (A) and (B). We also prefer answer choices that don't use extra words or phrases like *which* and *is when it*.

That leaves us with (D) as the right answer. Note that (D) is also the shortest answer, which is a strong indication that it's probably the correct choice.

www.grammatix.com

Question 10, page 414

Note that the given sentence is no good, since it uses a comma to separate two independent clauses. (E) is the correct answer choice here, and also the shortest answer. Note that other answer choices overuse the word *as*, which the SAT doesn't like. (D) doesn't use *as* too many times, but it messes up its verb tense when it uses *is* to refer to something that already happened.

Question 11, page 414

This one might be a little tricky. We can eliminate (A) right away because we know that we have to be careful about our modifier—the *some* aren't the ones with billions of tons left to be mined.

We can also tell that (D) is probably no good because it uses an *–ing* word that isn't necessary.

That leaves us with (B), (C). and (E) to consider. (B) and (C) introduce the word *because*, which we try to avoid in the right answer, but (C) and (E) also use the phrase *coal in billions of tons*, which is a very ugly usage of the preposition *in*—it would be a lot more natural to use *billions of tons of coal*.

So now we have to weigh things. It's pretty clear that (C) is no good, because it uses both *because* and that weird *in* phrase. Now we have a decision to make: is it better to choose (B) and leave the *because*, or better to choose (C) and use *coal in billions of tons*?

In this case, the *because* actually works, since the thing that comes after it really is the reason for something else in the sentence. On the other hand, the awkward use of *in* doesn't serve any purpose.

That makes it pretty clear that (B) is the best answer here.

We just saw how to improve sentences using the simple, repetitive application of basic concepts—we look for the key words and constructions that the SAT likes to test, and then we choose the answer choice that either avoids those key words or makes the best use of them. The more you do it, the easier it will become.

Conclusion

We've now discussed all the rules, patterns, and strategies for Improving Sentences questions in the SAT Writing Section, and you've seen them in action against actual SAT questions published by the College Board.

The processes that we used might seem repetitive and simplistic to you, but that's the whole point! Like we keep saying, we want to make the process of answering these questions as mechanical as possible—that's the way to excel on any standardized test.

Now we'll tackle the Identifying Sentence Errors Questions. You'll find they're fairly similar to the questions we've just worked on, but there are still some important differences.

General Overview of Identifying Sentence Errors on the SAT

The Identifying Sentence Errors Questions on the SAT are very similar to the Improving Sentences Questions in the sense that they test a limited number of concepts. But these questions are unique in that they don't ask you to rephrase anything—these questions are only interested in your ability to identify bad grammatical patterns. You don't have to worry about fixing any of the problems you see.

Each of these questions will present you with a single sentence. Several of the words and phrases in the sentence will be underlined. Your job is to find the part of the sentence that contains an error according to the SAT's idea of grammar, so if any of the underlined portions of the sentence is a bad pattern from the Writing Toolbox, you're going to mark it as the correct answer choice. If nothing is wrong with the sentence, you'll mark (E).

Just like the Improving Sentences Questions, these questions will start to seem very repetitive after you practice with them a little bit. So let's get started!

The Rules for Identifying Sentence Errors on the SAT

There are only a few rules for these questions that are worth pointing out, but they're very important, so don't forget them!

SAT Identifying Sentence Errors Rule 1: No Style Points

For these questions, you should think ONLY about grammar—don't worry about style like you did for the Improving Sentences Questions. That means you can't mark an answer choice just because you think there might be a better way to say it. Actually, there often IS a better way to say most of the things that appear in these questions, but your job is still only to find the things that are clearly grammatically wrong as far as the SAT is concerned.

SAT Identifying Sentence Errors Rule 2: No Deletions.

Sometimes you may be tempted to mark an answer choice because you think it should be deleted entirely. This isn't an option on the Identifying Sentence Errors Questions— the need to delete a selection isn't one of the "errors" you're allowed to identify on these questions.

The Hidden Pattern of Identifying Sentence Errors on the SAT

Just like the Improving Sentences Questions, the Identifying Sentence Errors questions only have one pattern that's worth mentioning (apart from the grammatical patterns that are discussed in the Writing Toolbox). Here it is:

Hidden Pattern 1: The Intervening Prepositional Phrase

Very often on these questions, you'll see that a prepositional phrase comes between a noun and its verb. Instead of agreeing with the correct noun, the verb will be made to agree with the noun in the prepositional phrase. A lot of students miss these questions because the verb agrees with the noun that's closest to it, so look out! Never forget that a verb has to agree with the noun that is its subject. (We realize this might be considered a grammatical pattern—in fact, we even talked about it in the Writing Toolbox. But it's so important, and it comes up so often on these questions, that we thought it was worth mentioning again.)

The SAT Identifying Sentence Errors Process

This is the process I recommend you follow when you're attacking SAT Identifying Sentence Errors Questions.

1. Read the entire prompt sentence.

You need to be able to place the underlined portion of the sentence in their proper context, so you have to read the entire sentence before you do anything else.

2. Focus on the underlined portions of the prompt sentence.

Remember that, as far as the SAT goes, only the underlined portions of the text can have something wrong with them—and, on top of that, only ONE underlined portion per sentence can be wrong.

3. Draw a line from each word in the underlined portions to the other words it is related to.

This step will connect all the words in the underlined portions of the text with the words in the rest of the sentence that they should modify or agree with. For example, if the pronoun *she* appears in an underlined portion of the sentence, draw a line connecting the word *she* with the noun that it's taking the place of. Then draw another line connecting *she* with the verb that goes with it. Use the concepts from the Toolbox to see which words in a sentence are related to each other—for example, a pronoun is related to the noun (or nouns) that it stands for, and a verb is related to its subject.

4. Look for an underlined word that doesn't fit the words it is related to.

Now that we've identified all the relationships between underlined and non-underlined words in the sentence, we check all those relationships to find the one relationship where a word doesn't fit the words it should be related to. For example, if the singular pronoun *she* is attached to the underlined plural verb-form *were*, then we know that *were* is used incorrectly, which makes it the right answer choice.

```
[when you've found an underlined portion of the sentence that
does not fit with the words it's related to, continue to step
5.]

[If you cannot find an underlined portion of the sentence that
does not fit with the words it's related to, go to step 6.]
```

5. Consider all the other underlined words.

Even after you think you've identified an error, continue checking each underlined word until you've looked at all of them. Never answer a multiple-choice question without considering every answer choice!

```
[If you still find only one underlined portion with an error,
go to step 8.]

[If you find two or more underlined portions with errors,
you've made a mistake—either start over or skip the question,
possibly coming back to it later.]
```

6. Consider the underlined portions of the text on their own.

It's possible that an underlined portion of the text may be incorrect by itself, without referring incorrectly to any other words in the sentence. For example, this can happen if a preposition is used incorrectly—the idiomatic expression *to be fed up with* might appear as *to be fed up of*, in which case the *of* part of the expression would make it incorrect, even if it doesn't refer to any other part of the sentence. You also have to look out for verb-forms that are mis-conjugated—the SAT might give you the underlined verb-form *has forgot*, in which case the *forgot* part of the sentence should appear as *forgotten*.

[If you've found one underlined portion of the sentence that is incorrect by itself, continue to step 8.]

[If you've found more than one underlined portion of the sentence that is incorrect by itself, you've made a mistake—there can only be one incorrect underlined portion of each sentence. Either start over or skip this question, possibly coming back to it later.]

[If you still haven't found anything wrong with the sentence, go to the step 7.]

7. Consider that there may be nothing wrong with the sentence.

Remember that not every sentence will contain an error. If you've considered all the underlined portions of the sentence and you haven't found one that has an error, then mark (E) and go on to the next question.

Don't forget that (E) will be the right answer as frequently, or infrequently, as it would in any other section; the SAT distributes correct answers the same way in every section. For more on that, see our discussion of SAT Misconception 9.

8. Re-read the sentence and mark your answer.

If you think there's only one underlined portion with an error, re-read the entire sentence to double-check yourself, and briefly reconsider each underlined portion.

[If you're sure of your answer, mark it and go on to the next question.]

[If you're not sure, either start over or skip the question, possibly returning to it later.]

SAT Identifying Sentence Errors Conclusion

We've just seen an entire approach to the Identifying Sentence Errors portion of the SAT Writing Section. Now, to show you that the process works, we'll try it out against actual SAT questions published by the College Board. Let's get started!

www.grammatix.com

Using the SAT Writing Process to Identify Sentence Errors

Now we'll try our hand at some real SAT questions from the College Board publication *The Official SAT Study Guide For the New SAT*.

Question 12, page 415

A couple of things are wrong with (C). Remember that the SAT doesn't like it when pronouns are used incorrectly, and there's no plural verb in the sentence that the plural pronoun *they* might be referring to. Also remember that the SAT doesn't like to use conjunctions unless they're serving the proper purpose, and the *and* in this sentence isn't really linking two connected ideas together.

Question 13, page 415

In this question, (C) is bad because it uses the wrong tense of the verb *to be*. The sentence uses the word *previous*, which indicates that the lifestyles no longer exist. Since that's the case, they should be referred to with *was*, not *is*. Also, note that all the other verbs in this sentence are in the past tense, and the SAT doesn't like to switch verb tenses in mid-sentence.

Question 14, page 415

(B) is wrong because the noun phrase here should be plural. Susan and Peter are two people, so they can't become one writer—they can only become separate writers. Remember that noun phrases on either side of a copular verb have to agree in number.

Question 15, page 415

We might be tempted to find something wrong with the last half of this sentence, but we have to remember that we can only choose the underlined portions of the sentence. In this case, it's pretty clear that you can't use the expression *either and*—instead, you should use *either or*. That makes (B) the right answer here.

Question 16, page 415

Remember from the toolbox that the SAT likes to see consistent pronoun usage. This sentence switches from *one* to *you*, which is no good. That means that (C) must be the correct answer here.

Question 17, page 415

This question gives us an example of an *and* construction. Remember that the SAT likes to see all the items joined by a conjunction phrased in the same way. The first two things in the construction are noun phrases (*company code*, *her initials*), but the last thing is a verb phrase (*enters*). The last item should be phrased as a noun, so (B) is the correct answer.

Question 18, page 415

This is the exact same situation that we just saw in question 17. Here, we have three things joined with the conjunction *and*. The first two items are nouns (*dancer, choreographer*), and the last is a verb (*collaborated*). That means (D) is the error in this question.

Question 19, page 416

This is another example of subject-verb disagreement. The subject of this sentence is the word plural noun *writings*, but the verb is in its singular form. The proper form of the verb would be *have continued*. That makes (B) the correct answer here.

Question 20, page 416

This is a relatively uncommon error on the SAT, asking us to identify the correct participle of the verb *to arise*. The given form is *has arose*, which is incorrect—when we have the helping verb *has*, we need the *–en* form of the main verb. The proper form is *has arisen*. (A) is the correct answer here.

Question 21, page 416

This is a sneaky one! Remember that the SAT doesn't like to switch tenses.

It might look like there's no error in this question. But the SAT mentions the "nineteenth century," which is in the past, and then talks about it with the verb-form *will be*, which is a future verb-form. The SAT doesn't like that, so (B) is the answer. Stay on your toes!

Question 22, page 416

This is the same problem we had in question 14—the SAT has switched numbers on us again. Notice that the plural noun *children* appears in connection with the singular noun phrase *a creative artist*—the two are joined by a copular verb. Those two phrases are inconsistent with each other, so one of them has to be wrong, which makes (D) the right answer.

Question 23, page 416

Once again, the SAT presents us with a singular noun and a plural verb—the noun *announcement* is paired with the verb from *were*. That means choice (C) is the correct answer here.

Question 24, page 416

Remember from the toolbox that we have to use the adverb-form of an adjective to describe anything that isn't a noun. In this sentence, the verb-form *designed* is modified by the adjective *clever*, when it should be modified by the form *cleverly*. That makes the correct answer to this question (B).

Question 25, page 416

Nothing in this sentence is incorrect. (A) gives us a singular form of the verb *sets* to match the singular form of the noun *company*. (B) gives us the adverb *probably* modifying the verb form *will be*. (C) starts a comparative with *as much by* that is then

---

paralleled by the phrase *as by*. (D) has the phrase *appraisal of*, which correctly uses the pronoun *of* to refer to the phrase *the market*. That makes the answer (E)—no error.

Question 26, page 416

This is another question where subject-verb agreement is missing. The singular verb-form *has become* appears with the plural subject *effects*. That makes (C) the answer here.

Question 27, page 417

This sentence doesn't have any errors in it. It might appear to some students that (C) is incorrect because it uses the plural verb-form *were* right next to the singular noun *Sam Houston*, but we have to remember that *were* in this sentence actually goes with the plural noun *individuals*. That makes it the correct form, so the answer here is (E).

Question 28, page 417

This is another relatively rare question type—a preposition used incorrectly in an idiom. Here, you have to recognize that *in* is the wrong preposition. The normal usage would be *preoccupation with*, so (C) is the correct answer.

Question 29, page 417

This one might be kind of tricky. Remember that we always have to be careful around *-ing* words on the SAT. The way this sentence is written, *Portuguese kings* is the phrase that would be doing the contrasting. But that's no good—the Portuguese kings can't contrast themselves with something; instead, some third party has to contrast the kings with other rulers. This is a pretty subtle error for most readers, but if we know that we always have to be extra suspicious of *-ing* words, we'll probably catch it. (A) is the right answer here.

Conclusion

We've now seen how to handle the Identifying Sentence Errors Questions on the SAT Writing Section. We've learned all about the rules, patterns, and processes for these questions, and we've seen real solutions worked out to real SAT questions published by the College Board.

As is the case with every other question type on the SAT, the more you work with these questions, the better you'll be able to answer them!

We only have one more type of multiple-choice question on the SAT left to talk about—the Improving Paragraphs Questions. Let's get going!

General Overview of Improving Paragraphs on the SAT Writing Section

For these questions, you'll be given a short, poorly-written composition. Every sentence in the composition is numbered. You'll be asked questions about how the composition could be improved. In general, the questions will ask about changes that could be made to individual sentences, ways to combine two sentences into one, or additions that could be made to individual paragraphs.

The Rule for Improving Paragraphs on the SAT

For the most part, the rules for Improving Paragraphs are essentially the same as the rules for Improving Sentences, because most of these questions are questions that could have appeared as Improving Sentences questions. The only questions you'll have to deal with in this section that are really new are the ones about adding and deleting sentences, so the rule below bears mentioning:

SAT Improving Paragraphs Rule 1: Simple Paragraphs

According to the SAT Writing Section, the best paragraphs are the ones that discuss the fewest number of topics. So whenever you're asked if a sentence should be deleted, choose to delete a sentence if the sentence introduces a topic that isn't mentioned elsewhere in the paragraph. And whenever you're asked if a sentence should be added, choose to add the sentence that introduces the fewest new concepts to the paragraph.

The SAT Improving Paragraphs Process

This is the recommended process for SAT Improving Paragraphs questions. Note that it incorporates the processes for the other SAT Writing Multiple Choice questions, and has some similarity to the Passage-Based Reading process.

1. Identify the type of question you're dealing with.

Remember that the Improving Paragraphs questions are sort of a combination of Improving Sentences questions and Passage-Based Reading questions. Many of the questions are almost exactly like Improving Sentences questions, and those can be answered using almost exactly the same approach as the normal Improving Sentences questions.

[If the question asks you to improve one or more sentences, or asks which version of one or more sentences would be better, proceed to the Step 2.]

[If the question asks about the role or function of a particular phrase, or if it asks anything about the author's strategic approach to the subject of the composition, go to step 3.]

[If the question asks anything else, proceed to step 4.]

2. Use the Improving Sentences approach, but be careful of small changes.

Use the Improving Sentences approach on the appropriate questions, but be careful—there are certain things you have to look out for. For example, there may not be an underlined portion of the sentence to fix; instead, any portion of the sentence might be changed, or the entire sentence could be replaced with a similar sentence that has the same effect. Still, the goal with these questions will be to find the optimal "SAT-ideal" sentence, the one that avoids the most "bad" patterns and uses the most "good" patterns from the chart in the Toolbox.

There's another very important difference you need to be aware of! For Improving Paragraphs questions, the best way to deal with a sentence may be to delete the sentence entirely! If you see that one answer choice is to delete the sentence in question, you'll need to use the process from Step 4 to determine whether that's the correct answer choice.

[If one answer choice is to delete the sentence, go through step 4 to see if that choice is correct.]

[If deleting the sentence isn't an option, mark the answer choice that creates the most "SAT-ideal" answer choice according to the process we used to answer Improving Sentences questions.]

3. Use the Passage-Based Reading Process to answer the question.

Questions that ask about an author's goal or strategy, or questions that ask about the relationships between one part of a composition and another, can be handled in the same way that we attacked the Passage-Based Reading Questions. As a quick refresher, remember that we NEVER succumb to subjectivity in answering a Passage-Based Reading Question, no matter how the prompt for the question is written!

www.grammatix.com

4. Use the appropriate toolbox concept to answer the question.

If an SAT Improving Paragraphs question is not essentially an Improving Sentences question, then it will ask you to apply a concept from the Writing Toolbox to the passage. These questions could be about the grammatical role of a particular word or phrase, or they could ask you to add or delete a sentence from a paragraph.

If the question asks about the role of a particular word or phrase, you can rely on the toolbox concepts about parts of speech, SAT-ideal usage, or whatever.

If the question asks you to add or delete a sentence from a paragraph, remember from the toolbox that the "SAT-ideal" paragraph discusses as few concepts as possible. This means that sentences that introduce extra concepts should be deleted or not added, while sentences that stick to the same concepts as the rest of the paragraph should be added or not deleted.

```
[If you can identify the correct answer choice after applying
the toolbox concepts, mark it and move on to the next
question.]
```

```
[If you can't identify one correct answer, either start over or
skip the question, possibly coming back to it later.]
```

SAT Improving Paragraphs Process Conclusion

You've probably noticed that the recommended process for answering these questions types is fairly short. That's because these questions are often extremely similar to the Improving Sentences and Passage-Based Reading Questions, so we were able to incorporate the process for those questions in Steps 2 and 3.

At any rate, let's take a look at these processes in action against real SAT questions published by the College Board!

Using the SAT Writing Process to Improve Paragraphs

In this section, we'll apply what we've learned to some real SAT questions from the College Board publication *The Official SAT Study Guide For the New SAT*.

Question 30, page 417

This question is similar to an Improving Sentences question, and we can use a similar approach to answer it. The change that brings this sentence closest to an ideal SAT sentence is (D), because it eliminates *arising*, which is an –*ing* word, without replacing it with another bad pattern from the Toolbox.

Question 31, page 418

This question is also basically an Improving Sentences question. The main problem with the original sentence has to do with usage. It doesn't make any sense to say that a person's goal is "if something happens." The goal in this sentence has to be a noun or an adjective, since the only verb is the copular verb-form *is*. (Remember from the toolbox that the *to* form of a verb—*to win*, in this case—can act like a noun.) The only option that correctly equates *goal* with a noun phrase is option (D).

Question 32, page 418

We need to establish the context of sentence 9 in order to answer this question. When we read the previous sentence in the paragraph, we see that the *it* in sentence 9 really refers to the entire phenomenon discussed in sentence 8. Since *strategy* is the only word in the answer choices that can describe the entire phenomenon in sentence 8, (A) is the correct answer here.

Question 33, page 418

This one might be tricky! When we're improving paragraphs, we can't just consider a given sentence on its own; we have to consider it in the context of the paragraph that it appears in. Sentence 6 is grammatically acceptable as it is, but it doesn't fit with the rest of the paragraph in which it appears—the paragraph is about the proper use of negative campaigning, and this sentence is about how the writer values character. That means the best thing to do with this sentence is to strike it entirely, so (B) is right—remember that the SAT likes paragraphs to have as few concepts as possible.

Question 34, page 418

Unlike sentence 6 from the previous question, sentence 14 fits the theme of its paragraph. So (B) isn't the right answer here—if we delete the sentence, its concepts would still appear elsewhere in the paragraph. Neither is (A), because this is a run-on sentence. (Remember from the toolbox that we can't separate two independent clauses with a comma.) (C) and (E) don't do anything to change the run-on nature of this sentence, but (D) does.

Wait a minute, though—if (D) is right, we'll be adding an –*ing* word into a sentence that didn't have one before. Isn't that the sort of thing the SAT usually hates? Yes, it is, but in this case the –*ing* word is used correctly. The way the sentence is written, the verb-form *saying* would be modifying the noun *media*. Is that what we want? Is the media really doing the saying in this sentence? Yes, it is—which means the usage is okay.

Question 35, page 418

For this question, we need to read the entire concluding paragraph in order to determine which answer choice fits it.

(A) is no good because the entire paragraph is about the negative aspects of this type of campaigning—if this sentence were put at the end of the paragraph, how would the writer explain the "bright side?"

(B) is no good because the word *this* wouldn't be referring to anything if this sentence were included—there are no "restrictions" mentioned anywhere in the essay.

(C) might be tempting because it includes the phrase *in conclusion*, which is often used by beginning writers to set off the final sentence of an essay. But the essay is not about media participation, so this sentence wouldn't actually conclude anything.

(D) is a bad ending because it tries to relate the idea of campaign cost to the writer's complaints about negative campaigning. Like (C), this answer choice has very little to do with the paragraph it would be added to.

(E) is the right answer. It only mentions two ideas, and both of them have already appeared in the paragraph—the first idea is the media's practice of spreading accusations, and the second idea is the negativity of political campaigning. When we add sentences, the SAT likes them to introduce as few concepts as possible, and this is the only choice that satisfies that requirement.

Conclusion

Now you've covered everything you need to know in order to answer Improving Paragraphs Questions on the Writing Section of the SAT. As long as you remember that these questions are mostly Improving Sentences and Passage-Based Reading Questions in disguise, you'll have no problems. At this point, we've covered every single type of multiple-choice question that appears on the SAT. Congratulations!

Make sure you don't stop reading now, though—we still have a few important points to consider.

No Two Ways About It: The Secret Reason Your SAT Score Is Lower Than It Should Be

I've spent more hours than I can count helping my students raise their SAT scores, and all of that time has helped me realize that there is a serious problem blocking most SAT-takers from realizing their full potential.

It's not a problem that has to do with strategy, memorization, timing, focus, or anything like that. This problem is at the root of the very nature of the SAT itself. And if you don't come to terms with it, your score can only be mediocre at best.

The problem is that the SAT only gives you one correct answer for each question, and the correct answer is totally, definitively, incontrovertibly the correct answer—there are no arguments to be made here.

A lot of students never realize this. In this Guide, we talk a lot about all the specific ways that the SAT is different from tests you take in high school. But I really want to pound this one difference into your head, because it will affect every single thing you do as you prepare for the test.

So I'm saying it again—read closely: SAT Multiple-Choice questions always have ONE, and only ONE, correct answer. Furthermore, the matter of which answer choice is the correct one is absolutely beyond disagreement. As surely as 2 and 2 make 4, not 5 or 3, every single SAT question can only be correctly answered in one way.

A Real-Life Example

Why is this such a big deal, you ask?

Imagine this common high school situation, which you've probably been through yourself. Your history teacher is going over the answers to a multiple-choice test with you. It's a test he wrote himself, and he wrote it just for your class. And as he's going through the test, he tells you that the answer to number 9 is choice (D). Half the class groans—they all marked (B). One of the students who marked (B) raises her hand and makes a convincing, compelling argument as to why she should get credit for marking (B). She explains that if you read the question a certain way, (B) and (D) are equally good answers. The teacher, who wants to be open-minded and fair, reconsiders the question, and decides that it's poorly written. In light of the student's argument, he can understand why (B) might have looked like the right answer. And, because he's fair, he announces that he'll give equal credit for both (B) and (D).

That sort of thing happens every day in high schools all across the country. It's the natural result of a system in which teachers have to write their own classes' exams, and don't have enough time to proof-read them or even test them out on sample classes in advance. Inevitably, some poorly written questions get past the teacher. The teacher corrects the problem later by giving credit as necessary, throwing questions out, or whatever.

What message does this send to students? Unfortunately, students come to believe that the answers to *all* tests are open for discussion and debate, that *all* questions are written by stressed-out teachers who work with specific students in mind, that *any* question is potentially flawed and open to interpretation.

Then, when these students take the SAT, things get crazy. They can never settle on anything, because they've been taught that the proper approach to a multiple-choice test is to look for any way at all to bend every answer until it's correct. They mark wrong answers left and right—usually they manage to eliminate one or two choices, and then the rest all seem equally correct, so they take a stab at each question and move on to the next.

As we know from our discussion on guessing, most of these students are wrong way more often than they think, and they lose a lot of points.

And the thing of it is, they never even realize what's holding them back.

Two Key Realizations

If you're going to do well on the SAT, you have to realize two things. First, you have to know that the SAT is a totally objective test, and that every single question has only one right answer. This is not like a test you take in high school. Those tests are written by one or two people, usually with very little review. The SAT, on the other hand, is written by teams of people. Before a question appears on the SAT, it's been reviewed by experts and tested on real test-takers. SAT questions are basically bullet-proof. No matter how much it might seem otherwise, every question on the SAT has only one good answer. You can't approach it like you approach a high school multiple-choice test, where anything goes and you'll get a chance to argue your point later on.

Once you come to accept that, the second thing you have to realize is that you—specifically YOU, the person reading this right now—can find the answer to every SAT question if you learn what to look for. You can. And with the right practice, you will.

So let's wrap this whole thing up nice and simple:
1. The only way to do really well on the SAT is to mark the correct answer to most of the questions on the test.
2. The only reliable way to mark the correct answer consistently is to be able to identify it consistently.
3. Before you can identify the correct answer consistently, you have to know and believe that there will always be one correct answer for every question—if you're open to the possibility that more than one answer will be correct, you won't be strict about eliminating answers by using the rules and patterns of the test.
4. Most students never realize this, and as a result they never maximize their performance. Instead, they treat the SAT like a regular high school test, which is a huge mistake for the reasons we just discussed.

Now that we've established this very important concept, we have to talk about something that comes up often in testing situations . . .

What Do You Do When It Looks Like There Might Be Two Right Answers To A Question?

Even though you know there can only be one answer to every SAT question, there will be times on the test when you think more than one answer might be correct. It happens to everybody. It happens to me, and it will happen to you. When it does happen, you must

www.grammatix.com

immediately recognize that you've done something wrong—you missed a key word in the question, you left off a minus sign, something like that.

There are two ways to fix this situation. One way is to cut your losses and go on to the next question, planning to return to the difficult question later on, when your head has cleared. This is my preferred approach.

The second way is to keep working on the difficult question. Try and figure out what might be causing the confusion while the question is still fresh in your mind, and resolve the issue right then and there. I'm not such a big fan of this one because I tend to find that my sub-conscious keeps working on the problem after I've moved on, and when I come back to it things are clearer. But some people find that moving on without answering a question just means they have to familiarize themselves with it all over again when they come back, and they prefer to stay focused on a particular question until they either find the right answer or decide to give up on it for good.

To see which type of person you are, just do what comes naturally, and experiment a little bit with both approaches.

Conclusion

The main thing to remember, for every question, is that there is only one correct answer. If you think you see more than one possible answer to a question, you're wrong. That's it—no discussion.

To become successful on the SAT, you MUST realize that every multiple-choice question on the SAT has exactly one correct answer, and you must train yourself to find the correct answer every time. This isn't a regular high school test. Don't treat it like one.

I realize, of course, that every once in a while an SAT question is successfully protested. This happens with such rarity that it's best for you, as a student, to proceed as though it never happened at all. The odds are overwhelmingly in favor of every SAT question you ever see being totally objective and valid.

Test Anxiety—Why You Have It And How To Beat It

Test anxiety is an important consideration for almost everyone who takes a standardized test. For that reason, it's something we have to talk about if we're going to help you get the highest score you possibly can.

I don't know about you, but I don't get excited about this kind of touchy-feely stuff. I'm not looking to peel back the layers of your psyche here. I just want to tell you how to deal with something that has to be addressed if you want to do your best on test day.

You Have Test Anxiety—This Means You

When I talk to students about test anxiety and how it can affect performance on the SAT, I tend to get two basic responses. The first response is a ready admission that the SAT is a scary thing. While I think that's an overreaction, at least it acknowledges that the SAT is something to be taken seriously. The second response is a much bigger problem—the second response is a complete denial that testing anxiety exists. This is a very, very dangerous attitude.

I'll admit that there might be some students for whom testing anxiety doesn't exist. I've never met one, but over a million people take the SAT every year, and somebody out there must not care about it at all. But if YOU are reading these words, it's for one of two reasons: either YOU actually want to read this, or someone who cares about you is forcing you to read this.

If you're reading this because you want to, then you know that you're planning to get something out of it. Whether you admit it or not, you're at least a little anxious about doing well—otherwise you'd be sleeping or something right now.

If you're reading this because someone who cares about you is making you do it, the first thing you should do is thank that person for taking an interest in your life. Not everybody has someone like that. The second thing you should do is accept that you're under some amount of pressure from the person who gave you this. Maybe you don't realize it, but you are. Trust me. And you're probably also under some amount of pressure from yourself. After all, nobody can MAKE anybody read anything—at some level, you're reading this because you want to, even if you only want to because someone is making you want to.

If you're feeling either of these pressures—internal or external—you should be prepared for them to show up in your life as some form of test anxiety. Or to put it another way, YOU HAVE TEST ANXIETY.

You do. Trust me on this.

Now, let's talk about how to handle it.

Making Test Anxiety Work For You

Whenever a high-pressure situation like the SAT presents itself, people tend to react in one of three ways: they ignore the pressure completely, they succumb to it and just plain freak out, or they handle it productively. Obviously, our best course of action is to turn test anxiety into something helpful.

www.grammatix.com

Test Anxiety—Why You Have It And How To Beat It

What do I mean by that? A lot of people dislike stress and anxiety, and do whatever they can to avoid it (or ignore it). But stress and anxiety exist for a very good reason—when we use them properly, they can propel us to new accomplishments. Ask anyone who's ever been chased—you run a lot faster when there's something behind you that pushes you to run. If you handle your stress the right way, you can let it become the thing that pushes you, instead of the thing that crushes you.

In order to do that, you need to do three simple things:

- Put the SAT in perspective.
- Use your anxiety to prepare.
- Harness your anxiety on test day.

Putting the SAT in perspective

Very few SAT-takers put the SAT in the proper perspective. The SAT is important, but it's not the end of your life. There are people all over the world who would do almost anything if they could write "Taking the SAT" near the top of their list of worries.

This is not to say that the SAT isn't important. It absolutely is. But it's just one test in your life—life will go on when the SAT is behind you, and there are much larger tests waiting for you in the future.

The proper amount of stress you should feel is something similar to the stress that an actor, athlete, or musician feels before the big event. You want to be nervous enough to feel a little jittery, but you never want to make the mistake of thinking that lives are in jeopardy.

There's another thing to keep in mind here, too. If you've had the good fortune to start taking the SAT early, you can take it multiple times—you can take it as many times as you want, and colleges don't care. (If a guidance counselor or someone else has told you different, see our section on well-intentioned people who lie to you about the SAT.)

Using your anxiety to prepare

Some students get so nervous about the SAT that they just prefer not to think about the test. Whenever it crosses their minds, they go watch TV or call a friend on the phone or something. In fact, this is the way they tend to deal with most stress—they try to ignore it. It's very normal. And, unfortunately, it's completely counter-productive.

The other way most people handle stress is to let it overwhelm them. I've had students who lost sleep because they stayed up at night crying about the SAT. It might sound a little extreme to you, unless you've been there yourself. This is another totally natural, and totally useless, way to handle stress.

So what should you do whenever you start to feel some SAT-related stress? Very simple. You should do something that helps you get ready for the SAT. Anything you want. Read some more of this Guide, or get out your copy of *The Official SAT Study Guide For The New SAT* and go through some sample questions. Practice writing your essay. Just do something—everything helps.

This lets you turn your nervousness into a positive, helpful force in your life. And it has two other benefits. First, your nervousness will go away pretty quickly once your mind realizes that you're taking concrete steps to fix the problem. Second, by turning your stress into preparation time, you're setting yourself up to handle your anxiety on test day—when that test-day anxiety rolls around, you can help get rid of it by reminding yourself that you've done your preparation, and that you're all set up to do the best you can possibly do.

www.grammatix.com

So let me boil it down: whenever you get nervous about the SAT, do something to help you prepare, and you'll earn the right not to be nervous anymore.

Using your anxiety on test day

You might not experience that much stress leading up to the test, but you'll definitely feel something on test day. The key to test-day stress is to make sure you channel it and force it to work in your favor.

First, make sure you're prepared for test day—have your pencils sharpened, put new batteries in your calculator, get your ID out, whatever. If you'll be driving yourself, make sure the car has gas. If somebody else will be driving you, make sure you know when and where you'll meet. Have your favorite breakfast before the test. Check out pages 12 and 13 of the College Board publication *The Official SAT Study Guide For The New SAT* before the test and make sure you have all the stuff you'll need. Remember, you want to get all of this squared away because it earns you the right to control your nervousness—you'll be able to tell yourself that you've done everything you needed to do.

That'll take care of your pre-test jitters. But what do you do when you get nervous while you're actually sitting in your desk, with your pencil shaking in your hand and thoughts of catastrophic failure racing through your head?

Simple. First, remind yourself about the proper perspective for the SAT. It deserves your respect, but it's absolutely not a life-and-death situation. Then, breathe in through your nose as deeply as you can, down into the pit of your stomach. Hold the air in your belly as long as you can, and breathe it out slowly through your mouth. It's impossible to stay nervous while you breathe deeply like this. (It IS possible to pass out while you're breathing deeply, though, so don't get carried away.) Taking a couple of deep breaths will get rid of any nervousness, and reminding yourself that the SAT is just a test—and that you've done everything you can do to beat it—will bring your mind back to the task at hand, which is beating the SAT in a methodical, systematic, mechanical way. Have at it.

Conclusion

SAT anxiety can creep up on you when you least expect it. As long as you can keep things in the proper perspective, and as long as you let your nervousness motivate you to prepare constructively, you can turn your anxiety into a force for good.

www.grammatix.com

On Being An SAT Machine

In this guide, we talk a lot about how to answer individual questions. Obviously, that's an important part of beating the SAT.

But you may have noticed that the processes and sample solutions get pretty repetitive pretty quickly. My students often complain, "After a while, doing these questions is just the same thing over and over . . ."

Some teachers might be insulted by that, but when I hear those magic words I just smile and say, "Exactly!" On a standardized test, when answering questions begins to feel thoughtless and automatic, you know you've made a huge improvement.

Standardized Tests Have Standardized Questions

It seems obvious, but a lot of people never realize that standardized tests must have standardized questions and standardized answers—otherwise, the results from one test day would have no relation to the results from another, and the test would be meaningless.

Never forget that the SAT is a test with rules and patterns that it has to follow, and once you start to unlock them you almost can't go wrong—it's almost like you turn into an SAT machine.

An SAT Machine At Work

One of the things I do for my live students is show them how I take a section of the test. I don't just show them the processes and strategies I use, although the processes and strategies are definitely very important. I also show them the speed and the attitude I use to approach the test. What do I mean by that?

When I'm taking the SAT, I have an inner dialogue going on in my head. It's very simple and straightforward. I'm reading each question, thinking briefly about what kind of question it is, then walking myself through the various steps described in these pages. It's all second nature to me. And if I get down to answer choices, I'm ruthless about cutting them out—as soon as I see something wrong with an answer, it's gone. Bam. Bam. Bam. Question. Bam. First step. Bam. Second step. Bam. Answer choices—bam, bam, bam, bam, bam. Next question. Bam. I keep it going until I'm done with the section, then check my answers. Unless I get myself confused or lose my concentration, I usually finish each section in well under half the allotted time.

When I take a test, there's no dilly-dallying or second-guessing. I'm prepared, and I know what to expect, because I know the SAT is ALWAYS THE SAME in all the important ways.

Becoming An SAT Machine

When most students take the SAT, they let their minds wander. They don't realize that every question has one clear answer, so they waste their time trying to justify every answer choice to themselves. They don't have set processes to rely on. They don't know the recurring rules and patterns to look for in every question. In other words, they don't take advantage of any of the gaping holes in the SAT. They're inefficient and unfocused, and their scores suffer for it.

So what do you do if you want to turn into a machine? The key thing is to remember that every question has one clear answer, and that you can find it. Stick to a game plan—know how to start in on any SAT question and keep going until you either arrive at the answer or decide to skip the question. Then just keep working your system all the way through the test. That's it. Don't get distracted, and rely on the test to give you the same sorts of questions you've seen before—don't worry, it will.

In a way, taking the SAT is similar to taking a driving test. You know in advance which skills you'll be asked to demonstrate and what rules you'll have to follow during the test; what you don't know is the specific situation you'll be in when you demonstrate each skill. Keep this in mind—stay flexible about applying what you know, but never forget that the range of things you can be asked to do is very limited.

Also, as weird as this sounds, strive for the SAT to be boring and repetitive. Some students look at the SAT as a way to be creative—what's the point of that? Find each answer, find it as quickly as possible, and reuse as much as you can from one question to the next. You'll be attacking the test in a systematic, methodical way before you know it—and that's the secret to real SAT success.

How To Use The College Board's Resources—And How Not To

I talk a lot about how you need to use College Board materials when you study. The College Board is the company that writes the SAT, and they're the only source of real SAT questions, which are absolutely essential if you're going to prepare intelligently.

But that doesn't mean that you should take everything the College Board says about the SAT as the truth. Trusting them too much would be a huge mistake.

Since I keep telling you to work with the College Board publication *The Official SAT Study Guide For The New SAT*, I'm worried that you might use that book in the wrong way, which can actually hurt you. I'm also worried that you might not use the College Board's online resources the very best way they can be used. So I've written this section of the Guide to explain exactly how you should use the College Board's materials. You have to use these materials properly if you want to do your best.

The Official SAT Study Guide For The New SAT

The first thing we'll look at is the proper way to use the College Board publication *The Official SAT Study Guide For The New SAT*. I've gone through the book page-by-page to explain the best way to approach it.

Third unnumbered page

The third unnumbered page of *The Official SAT Study Guide For The New SAT* contains a letter from Gaston Caperton, the President of the College Board. It includes this sentence:

> The best preparation for the SAT, and for college, is to take challenging courses.

This is laughable.

You should take challenging courses because they help you become a better person. They don't do anything at all to help you on the SAT, and it can be argued they don't do anything to help you in college either. We would all love it if they did, but they don't.

Advanced courses will teach you to write well, for example, while the SAT will reward the sort of writing that appears in our section on the SAT essay and in the College Board's own materials. Advanced courses will teach you higher math principles that will never appear on the SAT. Advanced courses will teach you to read and analyze a text like a literary critic, but the SAT will ask you to forego all subtlety and nuance and answer questions like a literalist.

The best way to prepare for the SAT is to get a bunch of sample tests written by the College Board and pull them apart on a technical level to see what they keep doing, and then learn how to do those things—and only those things—well. And that's what we've done in this book.

How To Use The College Board's Resources—And How Not To

Pages 3 – 6

These pages sketch out the format and background of the SAT and its development. You can read them if you want, but they're pretty useless as far as doing well on the test is concerned.

Pages 6 – 8

These pages explain the way the test is scored, and tell you how to interpret your score report. You'll definitely want to read them when you get your scores back, but if you haven't taken the test yet you can skip them for now.

Pages 9 – 10

This section explains the College Board's general theory about how you should prepare for the SAT. Ignore it.

Pages 10 – 11

This lays out the online resources that are available to you through the College Board's web site.

Pages 12 – 13

You MUST read these pages before test day. They lay out the things you'll need to take with you to the testing site.

Pages 13 – 15

You can pretty much ignore this part. You should especially ignore the part on page 14 that talks about the difficulty level of questions going from easy to hard within a section. This is a lie—you can prove it yourself by looking at a sample test. (See our section on lies and the SAT.)

Pages 15 – 17

These pages discuss the traditional guessing strategy. Skip them, and check out our section on SAT-guessing instead.

Pages 17 – 18

These pages give you the College Board's take on test anxiety. It might be useful to read this if you're looking for another perspective on the issue, but it isn't necessary.

Pages 20 – 26

These pages explain how to use the PSAT. They're useful as general information.

Pages 29 – 30

These pages give you the College Board's general advice on how to approach the Critical Reading Section. You can ignore it.

Pages 31 – 43

This section gives you some sample Sentence Completion Questions and lets you see the College Board's approach to them. It's different from the approach I recommend, and it doesn't take you step-by-step through the process of completing any question.

How To Use The College Board's Resources—And How Not To

Pages 44 – 48

These pages give you some sample Sentence Completion questions to practice on. Give them a shot if you want.

Pages 49 – 56

This section explains how the College Board suggests you approach Passage-Based Reading Questions. You are STRONGLY cautioned to ignore these pages—they tell you to approach the questions subjectively, which is not only bad advice but would be an impossible basis for the design of a standardized multiple-choice test.

Pages 57 – 96

These pages give you some sample questions. The first questions also have sample responses. Give these a look if you want; you might find them useful for practice.

Pages 99 – 102

These pages introduce you to the Writing Section of the SAT. Ignore them.

Pages 103 – 108

These pages explain how the College Board thinks you should approach the essay part of the SAT. Ignore them. Make sure you especially ignore the scoring guide on page 105—instead, use the advice in this guide and, if you can, play with essays on the automated scoring tool that the College Board provides online.

Pages 105 – 119

These pages provide several useless writing exercises. Do them if you feel like it, but don't expect them to help you on the SAT.

Pages 130 – 136

This section provides several sample essay responses. Compare them—and the sample essay responses that appear elsewhere in the book—to the scoring guide on page 105 and decide for yourself if that guide is any real indication of what scores high on the SAT.

Pages 137 – 139

These pages introduce the Identifying Sentence Errors questions, and give you the College Board's advice for approaching them. Some of the advice is okay, like looking for the mistakes that commonly appear on the test. But other advice is probably not that helpful. For example, you're advised to practice by reading sentences out loud—even though acceptable spoken English and acceptable written English are pretty different, and you won't be able to read aloud on test day.

Pages 139 – 144

These pages give you a chance to practice rewriting sentences—something you'll NEVER do on the SAT. This is pretty much a waste of your time.

Pages 145 – 152

This section gives you some sample questions to practice on. Go for it if you want.

How To Use The College Board's Resources—And How Not To

Pages 153 – 154
This section introduces you to the Improving Sentences Questions and gives you the College Board's advice for these questions. As usual, you can ignore it.

Pages 154 – 160
These pages have more writing exercises on them, which are pretty much a waste of time as far as the SAT is concerned. Skip them, unless you feel like doing them for some non-SAT-related fun.

Pages 161 – 168
These pages have samples for the Improving Sentences Questions. Do them if you feel like it; it can't hurt.

Pages 169 – 170
This section introduces you to the Improving Paragraphs questions. Again, it gives some pretty poor advice for these questions.

Pages 170 – 177
This section provides even more writing exercises that won't help you do multiple-choice questions at all.

Pages 178 – 188
These pages give you sample Improving Paragraphs Questions to work on.

Pages 189 – 214
These pages let you practice all the question types in the SAT Writing Section. Give them a shot if you feel like it. Make sure to check out the sample essays on pages 197 – 212, and remember to compare them to the scoring guide on page 105. You'll see that high-scoring essays have several grammatical errors, and that the most reliable way to predict an essay's score is to see how long it is.

Pages 216 – 225
These pages introduce you to the Math Section of the SAT, and give you the College Board's ideas about the best way to approach it. You can skip this if you feel like it.

Pages 227 – 302
These pages take you through all the mathematical concepts you'll need for the SAT. This section is similar in content to our own Math Toolbox, but the Toolbox is more simplified. If you don't understand a concept after looking at the Toolbox, or if you just want another explanation of something, then give this section a try. Just like the Toolbox, this part of *The Official SAT Study Guide For The New SAT* contains every single math concept you'll need on the SAT, so it's definitely worth your attention.

Pages 303 – 304
These pages explain how the College Board thinks you should approach multiple-choice questions on the SAT. Ignore this advice, especially the part on guessing (see my advice on guessing instead).

Pages 305 – 342

This section provides sample multiple-choice questions, some with explanations. Give them a shot.

Pages 343 – 346

You MUST read these pages. They'll explain how to fill out the grids for the Student-Produced Response Questions. They'll also remind you that it's okay to guess on these questions (and ONLY on these questions), because on these question there's no penalty for wrong answers.

Pages 347 – 364

These pages give you sample problems for the Student-Produced Response Questions on the SAT. Try them if you feel like it.

Pages 365 – 376

This section gives you general math questions to practice with. Try them out.

Pages 377 – 889

These pages are the meat of the College Board's book. They provide you with sample tests written by the test-maker, which you absolutely must use to get your score as high as possible.

The Official SAT Online Course

The College Board provides an online tool that you can use to get extra help on the test. It's called the Official SAT Online Course, and you can access it from www.collegeboard.com. It has a variety of tools that you might find useful as you apply to college, but by far the most important one is the online essay-grader.

The online essay-grading tool will allow you to enter your sample responses to the SAT's sample essay questions. More importantly, it allows you to "test" the rules of the essay section.

What do I mean by that? You can practice using the Essay Writing Process to make sure that you're getting it, because the online tool will score your writing automatically. You can even type in the sample essays that appear in *The Official SAT Study Guide For The New SAT* and have the tool score them—then go back to them and make small tweaks and changes to see how they affect the overall score. Try adding or deleting paragraphs, playing with transitions, swapping openings and closings, or whatever you want. The more you play with it, the more you'll get a sense of what the SAT Essay rewards and what it punishes.

Of course, the College Board's Official SAT Online Course also has other features— sample tests, lessons, study planners, and so on. Use these if you want. The sample tests will be especially helpful as you search for more official SAT questions after you exhaust the ones in *The Official SAT Study Guide For The New SAT*. The lessons and quizzes probably won't do you too much good, but they can't hurt either.

Conclusion

You simply can't get ready for the SAT if you don't use the sample tests and other resources provided by the College Board—they are the only source of real SAT questions on the entire planet.

But that doesn't mean you should take everything the College Board says at face value! Much of their advice reflects what they *wish* the SAT were like, not what it actually *is*. I hope this section of the Guide has shown you how to use the College Board's materials, and when to take their advice with a large grain of salt.

Are You Being Lied To? SAT Myths And Misconceptions

If you're taking the SAT, you're going to get a lot of advice from other people about the best way to approach the test. It might surprise you to know that the vast majority of SAT information that most people have access to is very, very incorrect. In my years of teaching people about the SAT, I've heard all sorts of myths, rumors, and lies about the test. Believe it or not, some of this misinformation comes from the College Board itself. Some of it comes from colleges, guidance counselors, and teachers. And still more comes from your friends and peers, and can even be found on Internet bulletin boards and in chat rooms. Most—but not all—of the people who spread this misinformation are well-intentioned, but that doesn't change the fact that bad information leads to lower test scores.

With that in mind, I've set out a few common SAT myths, misconceptions, and lies below. I'll also tell you how to verify any SAT rumor you might hear in the future.

How To Find The Truth About The SAT

One of the strangest things about all the SAT myths and rumors that are out there is that it's so easy to disprove them with a little research, but nobody takes the time. This is a huge mistake.

Make a commitment to yourself that you won't accept a single new piece of SAT advice from anyone, no matter the source, without checking it out for yourself to see if it's true. (Yes, I'm including my own advice here—I'm sure it stands up to the test, unlike most of the other SAT advice you'll encounter.)

How do you check it out? If the advice is related to the SAT itself, you can usually check to see if it's true by looking at some sample tests WRITTEN BY THE COLLEGE BOARD. Of course, you can get these by consulting your copy of *The Official SAT Study Guide For The New SAT*. Do NOT, under any circumstances, attempt to learn anything meaningful about the SAT by consulting a fake SAT test written by a large test prep company. They simply don't know how to write them correctly, and those fake tests are totally useless.

 Note that I'm not suggesting you take the College Board's advice about the SAT—I'm suggesting that you try out all SAT advice against the actual sample SATs prepared only by the College Board. The College Board is often wrong about its own test, as strange as that might sound. You can prove this by comparing the essay-scoring chart on page 105 of *The Official SAT Study Guide For The New SAT* to the actual high- and low-scoring essays that also appear in that book. What the College Board says it's grading for is not what actually appears in those essays.

If the advice is related to the way a particular college or university uses the SAT in its admissions process, one way to check it is to call up the school yourself and get the real answer, or visit the school's web site. The admissions people typically won't lie to you (notice I didn't say they'll NEVER lie to you). Unfortunately, admissions departments are not a perfect source of information. They may not always give you a straight answer about the role the SAT plays in their schools' selection processes. Fortunately, though, schools don't lie about their raw data—you can usually go to a school's web site and find out its median SAT scores and grade point averages for the previous year's admissions pool. If you can't get this information from the school itself, it may be available from a third-party ranking company.

So that's it—the only two places you should look to when you want to confirm something about the SAT are (1) the people who wrote the SAT, and (2) the schools you're interested in attending. That's it.

Notice who's not on that list: guidance counselors, friends, students and alumni of your target schools, even your parents. I'm not saying that all of these sources will be wrong all the time—I'm simply pointing out that these sources are never the final authority on the SAT. They might give you good information, but you'll never know for sure if it's good until you verify it with the College Board or with the schools you want to attend.

Now that we've established how to test all SAT-related advice, let's talk about some of the bad information that's out there.

Misinformation From The College Board

We've already talked about how to use the College Board's resources. As you'll see if you look at that section of the guide, much of the College Board's advice about taking the SAT is based on what can only be called a set of illusions about what the SAT really is and what it really does. (What's the rest of it based on? I can't tell, but most of it still isn't any good.) Let's take a look.

SAT Misconception 1: The SAT tests the skills that a good college student needs.

This is the major gimmick of the College Board. We've discussed what's wrong with this idea in almost every section of this guide: basically, there's no way that a standardized test can possibly measure a student's ability to perform in college, because college is a non-standardized environment. The essay section of the new SAT is probably the best proof of this fact.

This particular idea—the idea that the SAT actually measures something besides how well you do on the SAT—is very dangerous to SAT-takers. Since you're an SAT-taker, I want you to know the truth.

I can't tell you how many times a well-meaning student has told me that he wants to turn the SAT into a real intellectual challenge. He's going to prepare for it by taking advanced calculus courses in his junior year; he's going to read Cicero over the summer in the original Latin; he's going to volunteer twenty hours a week tutoring young children.

Now, all of those things are great. They'll make you a more intelligent person and a more attractive candidate in the admissions process. But they absolutely will NOT help you on the SAT, because the SAT is NOT an indication of how intelligent or well-rounded you are. The SAT is basically an indication of how well you can fill in the right bubbles on a piece of paper that gets fed into a machine.

So, then, what's the best way to get ready for the SAT? Attacking it on a technical level. Pulling it apart and finding all the hidden rules and patterns that dictate how the questions must be written. Establishing processes that let you attack every single question like a machine. Mastering the small list of mathematical and grammatical concepts that appear over and over again. In other words, the best way to beat the SAT is to follow the sort of approach outlined in this guide.

Give up the idea that the SAT tests college-related skills. We'd all like it to do that, but that isn't what it does. Read Cicero if you want to, but it won't help on the SAT much more than watching Sesame Street every morning.

Fact: The SAT is NOT a test of the skills you'll need in college. The best way to approach the SAT is to attack it on a technical level and turn yourself into an SAT machine.

SAT Misconception 2: "Educated" guessing is a good idea.

We've already covered this one in some depth. In case you missed it, though, check out the section on guessing.

Fact: Guessing on the SAT is NOT a good idea. Ever.

SAT Misconception 3: Hard questions appear at the end of each group of questions.

On page 14 of the *The Official SAT Study Guide For The New SAT*, this sentence appears:

> Within a group of questions, . . . the easier ones come first and
> the questions become more difficult as you move along.

This is another one of those things everybody knows about the SAT that isn't actually true. The College Board tells you it's true—so do most major test prep companies—but they have to know that it isn't, because they're the ones who put the tests together.

There are two ways we can prove that you won't necessarily find the tenth question in a group more difficult than the first question. First, turn to page 432 of *The Official SAT Study Guide For The New SAT* to see the difficulty levels that the College Board has assigned to all the questions for the first sample test in that book. You'll see that it's absolutely not true that every question is at least as difficult as the one before it. So that's one way to disprove this misconception.

But there's another, much stronger way to disprove it. The College Board assigns difficulty levels to questions based on how well other students do against the questions—for example, if most other people get a question right it's an easy question. That means that the difficulty ranking assigned by the College Board assumes that you're exactly like the average test-taker, which you aren't. If most test-takers haven't seen an Algebra problem in two years but you're in the middle of Algebra II, then an Algebra-based math problem is probably easier for you than it is for most other test-takers. And if they know all the words in the second sentence-completion question but you don't, then that question is harder for you than it is for them.

So there are two major flaws with this. First, the College Board doesn't even present its own questions in a strict rank order. Ssecond, and, more importantly, the ranking system it uses is completely meaningless anyway.

Fact: Any given SAT question might be easy or hard for you, regardless of whether it appears early or late in a group of questions.

Misinformation From Your Guidance Counselors

Most guidance counselors are well-intentioned, upstanding, good-hearted people. But they're usually pretty over-worked, and don't always go to the trouble of researching the SAT—they have lots of other stuff to take care of. This means they're usually working with SAT advice that's decades old—if it was ever any good at all.

SAT Misconception 4: You can't take the SAT more than 3 times.

I can't tell you how many times a student has told me that her guidance counselor told her not to take the SAT more than three times, because colleges supposedly looked down on students who did that.

This is completely untrue.

It IS true that some colleges advise students not to take the SAT more than three times, but this is only because they're trying to save you time and money. You see, the College Board released a study several years ago that showed that students' scores tended to level off after their third try on the SAT. Many colleges know about this study, and advise their applicants that taking the SAT more than three times might not be worth it.

But this is absolutely NOT the same thing as saying that colleges care how many times you take the SAT. They don't care at all.

Think about this from the colleges' perspectives. Most colleges have a very small team of admissions counselors who have to review a very large number of applications. The most selective schools rarely spend as much as ten minutes reviewing an application. They don't have the time or interest to count how many times you take the SAT—they're too busy scanning your resume, skimming your personal statement, and looking at all the other stuff in your file. In fact, at most colleges, the people who make the final decision about your prospects for admission don't even see your actual score report. That information has been previewed by an intern or clerk, and passed on in a more readable format to the decision-makers—usually without the number of times you've taken the test. (Don't believe me? Call up your target schools and ask.)

And even if colleges DID care about the number of times you take the SAT, why would they all universally agree that three times was the magic number? Does that make any sense at all?

Fact: Colleges only care how high your SAT score is, not how many times you've taken the test.

SAT Misconception 5: You should wait until you're a senior to take the SAT.

Many, many guidance counselors tell their students not to try the SAT until they're seniors. This is terrible advice.

The rationale for this advice is that students tend to score their highest as seniors in high school. This is certainly true, and there are a variety of reasons for it. At many schools, students might not have covered all the necessary math until the end of junior year. Students who are seniors are also more likely to have taken the PSAT as juniors.

Finally, most students who prepare intelligently tend to get better scores every time they take the SAT, and the last time most people take it is when they're seniors.

It would be a huge mistake, though, to assume that you'll get the same score as a senior regardless of whether you've taken the SAT before. Seniors tend to score higher because they've taken the test more times. That's it. If you want to score the highest you can, take the test as many times as possible, and learn from each attempt.

Fact: Assuming you have the time and money, the best time to take the SAT is the next available test date—and take it often after that, until you have the score you want.

SAT Misconception 6: A high SAT score costs time and money.

A lot of guidance counselors buy into the idea that you need help from some huge test prep company if you want to do well on the SAT, and that you'll need to spend dozens of hours prepping in addition to the thousands of dollars that a class might cost. This is absolutely not true.

At the barest minimum, all you need is a copy of the College Board publication *The Official SAT Study Guide For The New SAT*, which you can most likely get for free from a library. Study that long enough, take it apart analytically, and practice with it—you'll do better than most. If you want to save the time involved in all of that, just use the strategies from this Guide. With a copy of *The Official SAT Study Guide For The New SAT* and the Grammatix approach, you should be able to make massive strides forward in only a few hours.

Fact: SAT prep only needs to be time-consuming and expensive if you're not doing it right. The SAT is a simple test that requires a simple, mechanical approach.

Misinformation From Colleges

Believe it or not, colleges don't know that much about the SAT, even though they are the driving force that keeps it a popular test. After all, the latest changes to the SAT, which have made it more beatable than it ever was, were made largely at the request of the California University System—who thought they were turning the test into a better tool for measuring college-readiness. So be careful about what colleges say when it comes to the SAT.

SAT Misconception 7: Colleges don't care about the SAT.

I was actually taking a tour of Princeton University a few years ago when someone asked the admissions rep giving the tour what Princeton thought of the SAT. He said that Princeton didn't care at all about a student's SAT score.

We asked him to repeat himself, and he said again that a student's SAT score didn't matter to Princeton at all.

Now, I'm not ready to say this guy was lying. He knows more about Princeton's admissions process than I do. But let's look at some facts.

Princeton's own fact sheet for its 2004-2005 entering class shows that the middle 50% of those admitted for that year were in the top 1 percentile of all SAT-takers. That's awfully coincidental for a school that doesn't care about SAT scores, isn't it?

In addition, Princeton (like almost every other reputable school in America) takes the trouble of requiring students to submit SAT scores in the first place. Given that roughly

13,700 students applied in 2004, let's assume that it takes an average of five minutes for someone to receive a score report, process it for review, and pass it along to a decision-maker for final consideration in conjunction with the rest of an application (probably a low estimate, but go with me here). That would mean that Princeton spends approximately 1,100 hours every admissions cycle—several months of forty-hour work weeks—gathering data that it doesn't care about. Does that make any sense to you?

I'm only using Princeton as one example here. Lots of colleges tell their applicants they don't care about the SAT—but if that's true, why don't their numbers reflect it?

Fact: Colleges sure seem to spend a lot of time gathering SAT data from their students for it not to matter to them—and it's very coincidental that every college's pool of admitted students falls into a narrow SAT scoring band. The data suggests that most schools care about the SAT, even if they occasionally say otherwise.

Misinformation From Your Friends And Family

Now we're getting into a sore area. Most students are willing to accept that the information they get from the College Board, their guidance counselors, and the colleges themselves might not be that reliable. But now we're going to start talking about bad information you might be getting from the people closest to you, and that can hit home.

So let me repeat myself one more time: I'm not suggesting that your friends and family are lying to you, or that they're out to make you score low on the SAT. I'm just saying that they might be misinformed, and when they try to pass their advice on to you it might not actually be any good. As always, take the time to verify any advice by going to the source—real sample tests from the College Board.

The advice you tend to get from friends and family is a hodge-podge of strategies, study tips, and who knows what else, so this section might seem a little scattered. Also, it's just about impossible to cover all the rumors floating around out there, so we're only going to point out some of the major ones.

SAT Misconception 8: SAT Math stuff is for math people, and SAT Verbal stuff is for verbal people.

You hear people complain about this all the time. "I can't do well on the Math part of the SAT because I'm too creative," they'll say, or, "I'm too analytical to do well on subjective questions like Passage-Based Reading ones."

This isn't true at all. First of all, the human brain is too adaptable to be good at using only numbers or only words; if it weren't, we'd never survive. The recent trend in education that separates us all into "math people" and "verbal people," "audio learners" and "video learners," or whatever else, is a misapplication of good research that has wound up limiting a generation of students instead of tailoring learning to their needs. Except in the rarest of cases, people are not strictly good at either math or language.

But more importantly, the sections on the SAT don't really test Math and verbal skills. They just test general reasoning, using basic math and language concepts as the means to an end. In other words, the SAT Math Section isn't a Math test, the SAT Critical Reading Section isn't much of a reading test, and the SAT Writing Section certainly isn't a writing test. So even if you were only designed to do well on only Math or only language, it wouldn't matter on the SAT because the SAT doesn't test either of those things.

Want proof? Have you ever met someone who thought she was a "Math person" who scored hundreds of points lower on the Math section than on the other parts of the SAT? I meet people like this all the time. You might even be one of them.

If you are one of them, do yourself two favors. First, stop pigeon-holing yourself. You can be good at anything you want to be good at. Second, realize that the SAT isn't really a Math test or a language test, and just take it for what it is—a highly repetitive standardized test of basic skills and reasoning.

Fact: Anyone can do well on any part of the SAT—or on all of it—by attacking the test intelligently.

SAT Misconception 9: Answer choices are distributed evenly throughout each section.

A lot of students have told me they changed their answers on the SAT because the answer choices they originally liked didn't seem evenly distributed—it seemed like there were too many (A)s, or something ridiculous like that. When I ask them why they would worry about a thing like that, they say that somebody told them that the answer choices are always distributed evenly on the SAT.

This is partly true—over time, all the answer choices on the SAT are used equally. But within a section, the answer choices can be distributed quite unevenly. A section might clearly favor one, two, three, or four answer choices, or it might distribute its answer choices almost evenly. You never know.

Let's prove it. Turn to pages 432 and 433 in *The Official SAT Study Guide For The New SAT*. You'll see the same answers we used to examine Misconception 3. Let's see how often each answer choice appears in each section:

Section 2: 25%(A), 29%(B), 13%(C), 21%(D), 13%(E)
Section 5: 8%(A), 25%(B), 25%(C), 21%(D), 21%(E)
Section 8: 26%(A), 11%(B), 21%(C), 16%(D), 26%(E)
Section 3: 15%(A), 20%(B), 25%(C), 20%(D), 20%(E)
Section 6: 38%(A), 13%(B), 0%(C), 38%(D), 13%(E)
Section 9: 6%(A), 31%(B), 19%(C), 25%(D), 19%(E)
Section 7: 15%(A), 23%(B), 23%(C), 23%(D), 17%(E)
Section 10: 14%(A), 21%(B), 21%(C), 21%(D), 21%(E)

As you can see, there's absolutely no way to predict how many times a given answer choice should appear in a given section. So don't worry about the distribution of the answer choices you pick—just focus on trying to get every single question correct, and let the answer choices you select fall where they may.

Fact: Answer choices may or may not be distributed evenly on a given section. Don't worry about it.

SAT Misconception 10: You can time the SAT to get a higher score.

Some people will tell you that you should take the SAT at a particular time of year to get the highest possible score. The theory is based on the fact that the SAT is a norm-based test, which means that when you take it you're compared to other test-takers, not to some objective standard. So the idea, frankly speaking, is to try to take the test at the time of year when the people taking it with you are likely to be the stupidest.

www.grammatix.com

This idea can't possibly work, for a variety of reasons. The simplest reason is that you can't predict when the weaker test-takers are more likely to take the test. Some people say they're more likely to take the test late in the academic year, because they're procrastinators. Some people think they take it early in their senior years so that they'll just barely make the admissions cutoffs. But even if one of these theories could be proven (they can't), you'd be ignoring the fact that the best test-takers are the ones who take the test often and early—and they're likely to be in the mix at any given point. So even if there were a time of year when the weakest test-takers took the test, the strongest test-takers are just as likely to be out in full force on any given date as they are on any other.

(Of course, there are other reasons why this idea is doomed to failure—the sample size is too large, for one thing, and statistical norming doesn't only take into account the people who take the test with you, for another. But don't worry about that for now—just remember that you can't time the test.)

Fact: It's impossible to time the SAT for a variety of reasons. Just take it when you have the time and money, and take it as often as you feel comfortable.

Conclusion

We've just gone through ten common SAT misconceptions. There are a lot more of them out there—you're certain to run across more of them as you continue to prepare. Just remember that you should always double-check everything you hear. You don't want to get a lower score than you deserve because you followed some bad advice.

Farewell

I'd like to thank you for taking the time and effort to read my SAT advice. I hope, for both our sakes, we've been able to raise your score. If you haven't hit the score you want yet, please keep it up—you'll be glad you did.

You can send me any questions, concerns, or advice you might have at this email address: mbarrett@grammatix.com . I look forward to fielding your questions and hearing about your success.

I'm going to leave you with some words written by my younger brother, who scored a perfect 1600 on the old version of the SAT by following the Grammatix strategies for that version of the test. He's written an essay on the determination and dedication that sets high scorers apart. I encourage you to read it—it's not very long, and it sure says a lot.

Thanks again, and congratulations in advance!

Mike Barrett, President
Grammatix, Inc.

Mike is an accomplished instructor and public speaker. He's available to speak to your group about education, standardized testing, and related subjects. Contact him at mbarrett@grammatix.com

Bonus Appendix

Closing the Gap

An elite scorer tells you how to prepare

My name is Patrick Barrett, and I achieved a perfect score on the SAT[*].

A perfect score on the SAT requires a deeper knowledge of the test, a more precise understanding of its methods, and a little (not much) more effort. Conversely, most people who score below average, or below what they expected, do so because they were uninformed (or, worse, misinformed) about the test. This short section will show you the way to the next level of test-taking by outlining key elements of your preparation.

If you apply the following advice, however basic it may seem, you will go much further toward your full potential.

A perfect score of 1600 on the pre-2005 version of the SAT.

The Nature of Elite Scores

Imagine a hypothetical test with 100 questions of varying difficulty on various subjects. If you needed to answer any one question correctly, in most instances it would not be too difficult to do so. You could probably find one question somewhere that you felt comfortable with.

Now imagine that you have answered ninety questions correctly, and you want to get one more of the remaining ten. The odds are good that you have answered all of the easy questions. All that are left are the ones you skipped, and now you are stuck. Imagine that you wanted to get nine of the ten remaining question, or even all ten.

My point is this: The more you improve, the harder it is to improve, and the more you succeed, the rarer your opportunities for future success become. The more questions you master, the closer you come to having to deal with the hardest questions and the question types that you might not like. You just have to get through it.

Having The Right Attitude.

Your attitude is an important factor in preparing for the SAT.

Accountability

If you want a good score, *you* have to do it. This is the most obvious thing you'll read in this Guide, but it is also the most important. Every other strategy or attitude will fail you unless you take full accountability for your performance.

Many people feel that they have performance anxiety that makes them bad test-takers. Others think the test is biased against them. These people may be absolutely correct, but that will not help them improve their scores. The only thing that will help you improve is hard work.

Thinking about nonspecific problems that you cannot fix will only distract you from other weaknesses that you *can* fix. When you conquer all the problems you can pinpoint, you may be surprised to find that there are no others left to deal with.

Persistence

You will fail in some way, however small or large, over the course of your preparation for this test. Everyone does. However, failure is as impermanent as you want it to be. If you are willing to work for it, every failure is literally another opportunity to succeed in the future

Because this is the case, as stated above, you can take the test as many times as it is administered before your applications are due. You can take it ten times or more if you have started early enough. Do not consciously allow failure, but do not be discouraged if and when it happens. Only remember to keep working until you are satisfied.

www.grammatix.com

Practicing the test

Performing on the SAT, like any other skill, becomes easier if you practice it.

Choosing Your Pace

You will need some amount of some kind of practice; the kind and amount depend on how well you've done so far, in which areas, and how well you want to do in the future.

First, at the very least, everyone should become familiar with the question types by reading this Guide and looking through a copy of the College Board Publication *The Official SAT Study Guide For The New SAT*. Most people should take a fake, timed SAT in a reasonably simulated, timed environment. However, if you have started early enough, and you feel comfortable with it, you can just sign up for the test and take it once in order to get a realistic idea of your performance. In either case, the point is to find out where you stand, and which areas need work.

Once you grade your test or receive your score report, you can read it to find out how you performed in which areas. Obviously, you want to pick out the areas where you are not satisfied and work more on them with this Guide and *The Official SAT Study Guide For The New SAT*. The way you work on them is up to you. You can do one problem at a time while reading through the steps in this Guide, you can take one section of your trouble area at a time, or you can go ahead and take the full test.

However, you need to be sure to time yourself when you work up to full sections or tests, and you have to be responsible in your practice. If you don't feel like you are practicing enough, or you are not improving, then you need to put in more time, or go back to basics with the Question-Type Guides. Just keep working away at it. You get results depending on the work you put in, so if you want an elite score, remember: Work smarter *and* harder.

Assessing Weakness

As you practice you will notice certain areas of the test that seem to give you particular trouble. Take note, and work harder on those sections. There is no "I can't do it"—the information you need is there in every question, just learn to see it and use it. Don't be tempted to convince yourself that one question type is just too hard or flawed or has some other problem. You can do them all if you will only work on it.

When you do start to notice problem areas, see them as places where you have not yet succeeded, not places where you won't or can't succeed. Learn the difference between recognizing weakness and expecting failure.

Making it count

You can spend all the time in the world practicing, but if it's mindless practice, then you won't improve. Practice actively and intelligently. Don't try to look up every word in the verbal section and memorize its meaning, but if you feel like you keep seeing a word with which you are unfamiliar, go ahead and look it up and be sure you understand what it means; the odds aren't bad that you'll see it again somewhere.

However, if there is a word in the math section that you don't understand, look it up every time. This isn't as extreme, since there are far fewer of them in math than in verbal, but you cannot answer a math question without knowing the vocabulary.

Also, feel free to come up with your own tricks while practicing, but if your tricks don't work every time, then don't rely on them. When you've mastered all the techniques, you shouldn't just be right all the time; you should know that you're right, know why you're right, and know how you're right—every time. Remember: if you're not getting 800s (or whatever your goal is) in practice, you probably won't get them on the real test.

Parting advice

If you're putting in all this extra effort, then you have a goal, whatever it is. Keep that goal in mind. Let it motivate you to continue to work even when you don't want to. If you get your score report and you are not satisfied, think of it as a progress report and let your goal keep you working. Repeat this entire process thoroughly in order to optimize your improvement.

At the same time, treat each test as the real thing, because it is. Don't take a test thinking only that it will help you know what to do better later. It will, but always shoot for your goal or else you might not do as well as you can. Strive to do your best, *always*.